Democracy in Crisis

Democracy in Crisis

The Neoliberal Roots of Popular Unrest

Boris Vormann and Christian Lammert

Translated by Susan H. Gillespie

PENN

UNIVERSITY OF PENNSYLVANIA PRESS

PHILADELPHIA

Published by
University of Pennsylvania Press
Philadelphia, Pennsylvania 19104-4112

www.upenn.edu/pennpress

Printed in the United States of America on acid-free paper
10 9 8 7 6 5 4 3 2 1

A catalogue record for this book is available from the Library of Congress.
ISBN 978-0-8122-5163-0

To Janet and Lara

Contents

Preface

Publishing an updated English-language version of this book in 2019 has a decisive advantage over the German publication that came out just a short time after the Brexit vote and Donald Trump's election victory: we don't have to spend much effort convincing readers that we are in a deep crisis. Two years on, pessimism and doomsday scenarios are ubiquitous, and crisis metaphors dominate political debates and media discourses. Prominent political figures warn of resurgent nationalism, even fascism, and societies are divided by deep cleavages that seem almost impossible to bridge. And yet, we think there is an alternative to defeatism and inner exile. It rests on taking stock of the crisis we are facing to envisage more hopeful political futures.

What exactly is this crisis about? Answering this question has become more difficult since the first edition of our book appeared. The more the crisis has metamorphosed over time, the more its causes seem disjointed and indecipherable. On the book market, national perspectives and country-by-country analyses dominate, and, as we would contend, distract our view from more common, cross-national problems. A case in point: Germans often see the crisis of democracy as a result of a decade and a half of Angela Merkel, a partially failed reunification, institutional shortcomings, and illiberal remnants from a predemocratic past. But if that were so, if this particular crisis really were a German phenomenon, arising from distinct traditions and path dependencies alone, why is there a National Front in France that easily made it into the last round of the presidential elections, and why was there a referendum for Brexit, at very much the same time?

Also, a pan-European view wouldn't be much more helpful. One could of course point to the refugee crisis as the common denominator of Europe's predicament. Obviously, if you look at the programs of right-wing extremist parties across Europe, that certainly seems to be a rallying point. But if that were the sole cause of the crisis of democracy, why do we see similar developments in the United States, where such an influx of refugees never took place? Vice versa, if Hillary Clinton lost to Trump only because of Russian interference or the Electoral College, why the similarities with Europe? Are these parallel developments of polarization and anti-establishment backlash across these contexts a coincidence? To put this question differently: Why do we see Trumpism—as a new political form that by far exceeds Trump—on both sides of the Atlantic?

There seems to be something larger at stake that transcends individual national and even continental contexts. In this book, we speak of "crisis" in the singular for a reason: what we are arguing is that in the transatlantic context, we are experiencing variations on a theme. The language of "populism," by contrast, can distort our understanding of what is going on. It is a symptom of a much deeper crisis of liberal democracy. Overcoming this predicament will require the reinvention of the political sphere, a rejuvenation of its institutions and mechanisms of responsiveness—and a new, nontechnocratic debate about the collective futures of our societies: urban, regional, national, and global. If the crisis of liberal democracy, despite all the risks that it poses, has one advantage, it binds back into the political process constituencies that had opted out before. It might animate those whom the democratic deficits of our institutions have led into political apathy. It should be the work of politicians, but just as much of civil society and academia, to harness this reinvigorated debate. We can use its momentum to discuss a range of deep transformations that our societies are facing in terms of rapidly changing labor markets, climate change, and potentially emancipatory uses of new technologies.

The crisis of liberal democracy is profound. Rebuilding trust in democratic institutions will be a long-term task. But this is also a moment to think big. Yes, incremental improvements are possible and necessary. They are also much needed, given deep cynicism in the political process. But what incites the imagination is not campaign finance reform. Moreover, simply calling out Trumpism as chauvinistic and racist is necessary but won't do the trick. A politics of indignation will not suffice to counter a politics of resentment. There is an urgent need to develop economic and social policy visions beyond anti-Trumpism: something neither the Democrats in the United States nor the Social Democrats in Germany have been very successful at articulating since 2016, even though some more recent developments seem promising. If our analysis in

No Alternatives?

Washington, D.C., January 20, 2017: Donald Trump steps up to the podium on the west front of the U.S. Capitol. Behind him are previous presidents and the establishment, objects of the newly elected president's scorn during preceding months. In front of him stands a crowd of curious onlookers who get to hear a highly unusual inaugural address. Unusual? New presidents normally use these speeches to put the trench warfare of the campaign behind them, heal the divisions in the country, and unite its people to take on current challenges. Every American president of the twentieth century has faithfully performed this reconciliation ritual, which is intended to put the commander in chief's personal mandate at the service of the common good and insert it into the narrative of a glorious national history. Thanking the former incumbent and paying tribute to the peaceful transfer of democratic power are firmly anchored in the protocol of the handover of authority. Actually, the addresses are nothing special, mostly a lot of political symbolism.

That's what people were expecting. But Trump had other plans. With the very first sentences of his speech, after a cursory thank-you to his predecessor Barack Obama, Trump emphasized the special significance of his presidency: "Because today we are not merely transferring power from one administration to another, or from one party to another—but we are transferring power from Washington, D.C., and giving it back to you, the American people." Obama's expression, which could be observed on camera during much of the speech, clouded over, at least by the time the following sentences were uttered: "For too long, a small group in our nation's capital has reaped the rewards of government while the people have borne the cost. Washington flourished—but the people did not share in its wealth."[1]

That Trump was no ordinary presidential candidate was already well known. But many people hoped the office would quickly put its stamp on him. Trump's inaugural address, in the capital, was a first indication that these hopes would be in vain. Moreover, at that time there were already signs that the crisis of democracy would not be confined to the United States. Other nationalists were also seeing that their hour had come. Trump favorite Nigel Farage, the former head of the British right-wing U.K. Independence Party, was also in Washington for the inauguration. He saw Trump's success as an omen for renationalization on the European side of the Atlantic. According to Farage, "Brexit was the first chink in the wall, and Trump's victory was another Brexit from the global scene." In turn, this dynamic would find further expression in Europe, for example, in the Italian referendum in which "the people took a bazooka and fired a whole salvo at the pro-E.U. establishment, and thus gave voice to those who were defending themselves against the centralization of power and against Brussels's rigidity and its rules."[2]

So it was not terribly surprising, the day after Trump's speech, as the Who's Who of European right-wing populism met in Koblenz, Germany, to evoke their common purpose, that Marine Le Pen, the leader of the National Front (now the National Rally) in France, spoke triumphantly of 2017 as the year in which "the peoples on the European continent are waking up." She called out to the audience, which throughout her speech was constantly chanting, "Merkel must go, Merkel must go," saying that "we are living through the death of one world and the birth of a new one."[3] For Le Pen, and more generally for this rebirth of nationalism in Europe, the element of fear is central, as it is for Trump. Whether it is fear of Islamization, which supposedly makes women even in proud Germany "afraid to show their blonde hair"—as Dutch demagogue Geert Wilders, leader of the Party of Freedom, emphasized in Koblenz[4]—or fear of the European Union, which "started out regulating the curve of cucumbers" and ultimately "wants to regulate our thoughts," as Frauke Petry, party spokesperson of Alternative für Deutschland (Alternative for Germany) at the time, asserted.[5]

But where does this openness to populists come from? How could the growing strength of the right-wing nationalists come to pass? So suddenly? Out of nowhere? There is only one thing most pundits on both sides of the Atlantic seemed to agree on after the turbulent spring of 2017: they would not have thought the rise of the neonationalists was possible.

Chapter 1

How Did It Happen?

Let us dial back, then, to the evening after the 2016 U.S. presidential election. On the night of November 8, 2016, as the results of the election were gradually becoming clear, the media showed images that could hardly have been more different. On one side, in a windowless auditorium in midtown Manhattan, we see a small band of frenetic Trump supporters in red baseball caps bearing the slogan "Make America Great Again." The international press is not allowed into the room to follow the improvised victory speech of the surprised president-elect as he addresses the not-very-large group of his supporters. A few miles away, we observe a completely different picture. In the pompous Jacob K. Javits Convention Center, to the cheerful accompaniment of a brass band, Hillary Clinton followers, confident of victory, are forced to witness the loss of one state after another—North Carolina, then Wisconsin, then Michigan—until they are finally asked by campaign chairman John Podesta to leave the room without having caught a glimpse of their candidate. The unexpected defeat in the contest with a grotesque outsider had hit her too hard, it was rumored in the days that followed.

Not one of them saw Trump coming—not even Trump. Days later, Hillary Clinton was still in shock. None of the experts had given the eccentric real-estate billionaire even a sliver of a chance. At the beginning of the campaign, members of Clinton's team went so far as to hope for Trump as the opponent: this is how little he was seen as serious competition. Like everyone else, Nate Silver, the numbers guru for political predictions, was also miles off with his prognoses. Even during the night of the election, on the front pages of established media, such as the *New York Times* and *Politico*, the probability that Clinton would win was calculated at 90 percent.

And yet Trump won.

But was the electoral outcome actually so surprising? Months before, with Brexit, a very similar pattern could have been observed. There, too, everything seemed clear on the evening before the decision. Next morning came the unexpected electoral result, the shock. The neonationalists of the U.K. Independence Party were jubilant. Elsewhere, too, a very similar departure from the status quo was occurring. In France, the extreme right party National Front, under the leadership of Marine Le Pen, reached the second round of the presidential election. The plot thickened. And the general impression of a crisis of democracy becomes even stronger if we look beyond the borders of European nations and the United States, the countries that in the past have often boasted of their democratic tradition. Further east, for some time now, there has been talk of so-called sovereign democracy, in Russia, or illiberal democracy, in Prime Minister Viktor Orbán's Hungary. Turkey, under Recep Tayyip Erdogan, has also turned away from its own democratic tradition. Some people, looking at China's example, even think that economic growth is not compatible with democracy anyway—that it is quite possible to do without the latter, in everyone's interest.

What is new now, though, is that the United States and member states of the European Union—countries that not long ago would still have been described as functioning, even exemplary democracies—have also stumbled. The crisis that is evident in both places is an expression of divided, increasingly unequal societies that feel decoupled from the advantages of globalization. In a number of countries, the crisis of democracy is directly expressed as the centralization of power in the hands of individual personalities. Most of these nations show a lack of accountability by elites to their electorate. In the transatlantic context, there is a desire for strong personalities who promise a way out of the deeply felt economic and social crisis. In the United States, this took the form of Trump on the conservative side and Bernie Sanders on the progressive side. Both men mobilized supporters based on a critique of the political establishment and demands for thoroughgoing political change. Sanders even spoke of a "political revolution" and called himself a socialist—something that in the United States, a country that supposedly never wanted to have anything to do with socialism, would normally be considered certain political suicide.[6]

But where is this crisis actually to be found? Is the indignation just an allergic reaction by the educated class and left-leaning intellectuals to the fact that their favored candidates did not emerge victorious in the election? Isn't the whole meaning of democracy that there is a pluralism of opinions? Are Trump and Brexit, to put it differently, not proof positive that democracy is working?

In fact, we are not talking primarily about an institutional crisis. Trump was democratically elected, the established control mechanisms (still) seem to be functioning, and there is political resistance to his absolutist claims. That is correct. And yet it is quite clear that we are facing a tangible crisis of democracy—one, however, that can be understood only if we look further back than the events of the last couple of years. The causes of the crisis of democracy are much more profound than the rise of various demagogues, autocrats, and oligarchs. That triumphal procession of populists is a symptom of the crisis, not its cause. This is decisive. They are the consequence of a deeper-lying crisis of democracy. The failure, then, is not only to be blamed on those people who are now voting for antidemocratic politicians, as though they had just been too simple-minded to understand how good free markets had actually been for them. It must be sought in policies that over the past decades have become increasingly removed from the interests of broad segments of society.

The Contours of the Crisis

Our thesis is as simple as it is radical. We argue that the core of the crisis lies in a *politics of no alternatives*. Over the last four decades, this politics has put the market above all other social and political relations. It starts from the assumption that the welfare of the public is best served by the efficiency of private actors. It disparages public goods as a waste of taxpayer dollars and regards state intervention as clumsy interference. Economic and social policy, says the politics of no alternatives, must adapt to the givens of globalization. In this brave new world of the markets, everyone is responsible for himself or herself.

On one hand, therefore, we are talking about a crisis of political practice. In the name of democracy, the markets were unleashed, first in the United States and Great Britain. After the fall of the Berlin Wall, other countries in Europe and the world followed suit and ceded parts of their educational, welfare, and health care systems to the private sector. In a series of shocks, the thought experiments of neoliberal trailblazers at the University of Chicago—the so-called Chicago Boys—were put into practice.[7] The markets were actually supposed to block state paternalism and put an end, once and for all, to the fascism and totalitarianism of the twentieth century. But in fragmented societies, where private interests rule the day and public welfare has begun to break down, new dangers for democracy have recently sprung up.

Social mobility, the promise of social advancement, was the first and perhaps the most important victim of the triumphal march of the markets over all things political and social. Another piece of collateral damage was the responsiveness of elected representatives. Politics, these days, often listens only to the interests of powerful private actors, while all the other voices in society are rarely heard anymore. Feeling left behind and no longer being taken seriously—this widespread impression is the central consequence of the politics of no alternatives, for which purchasing power and growth have become the mantra of public policy. This politics creates the resentment and anger that are aimed at those on top and that lead to a search for alternatives at almost any cost, alternatives that obviously also include undemocratic ones.

A number of shocks recently served as catalysts for this long-term development on both sides of the Atlantic: the financial crisis of 2008, in which despite public budget deficits there was enough money to bail out banks and creditors; in Europe, additionally, the crisis of the euro, which shed a harsh light on the differences between northern and southern Europe; terrorism, which fanned fears of countries further opening up to the world; and the refugee crisis, which was linked to terror and made the closing off of democratic societies more acute. To these were added ambitious right-wing nationalists, who in Germany did not hesitate to use violence and burn down refugee housing, in France even seemed to have become socially acceptable, and in the United States actually managed to shove their way into the highest echelons of government.

The crisis of political practice is essentially a consequence of the shift of all political decision-making to the sphere of private value maximization. Behind the politics of no alternatives, therefore, there also stands the depoliticization of democratic processes. There is only one good and possible set of policies, and all we need are the right experts to turn it into reality. Nowadays, however, it seems that for large segments of society this type of technocratic government is no longer tolerable. The polarization on both the right and the left sides of the political spectrum—for on the left, Bernie Sanders in the United States, the political party Podemos in Spain, and the coalition Syriza in Greece are also expressions of the crisis of democracy—reflects this frustration with the status quo. Electorates and members of civil society long for new politicians and policies. They long for them, as evidenced by the increasing frequency of crises in recent years, insistently and now.

Liberalism out of Balance

Despite all the grounds for concern, in the midst of the crisis, the hope for another world is also growing. After years of political apathy in the old democracies on both sides of the Atlantic, civil society is in motion. Participation in elections and demonstrations is rising. The polities of Western democracies may have been corroded by the centrifugal force of the markets, but in the various different national

contexts an emancipatory politics is also germinating—
the first rough outlines of an alternative to no alternatives.
The crisis of established democracies is seen by some as a
restoration of political diehards, a chauvinistic reaction to
the liberalization of recent decades.[8] But is it also, perhaps,
the emergence of a movement toward more democratic
societies? The answer to this question is not yet decided,
and it depends first on the role that, going forward, will be
assigned to politics and democratic institutions.

For this reason, it is also essential to take a look at
the worldview that has led to the crisis of democracy. For
the crisis is an ideological one as well. The politics of no
alternatives has its parallel in distorted liberal thinking—
an approach that over the last few decades has degenerated into groupthink among political and economic elites.
Thus, anyone who wants to get to the bottom of the crisis
of democracy cannot avoid dealing with the political tradition of liberalism, which is at the heart of this orthodoxy.
But the concept can be confusing, not least of all because
it is applied differently in the United States and Europe. In
Germany, people tend to associate liberalism with membership in the business-friendly Free Democratic Party,
while in the United States a "liberal" is a Democrat, in
other words, someone who in Europe would more likely
be a Social Democrat. Confused yet? It gets even more
complicated when the already overheated term *neoliberalism* is invoked, generally as a label for the market-friendly
policies of the last few decades.

Liberalism refers simultaneously to a political philosophy, an ideology, and a political practice. This ambigu-
ity is responsible for most of the confusion. When we use
the term *liberalism* in this book, we mean something very

precise: a worldview that, in principle, accords high priority to the market mechanism as a means of preventing the centralization of state power and protecting the rights of individuals. This idea emerged in eighteenth-century Europe, and—this is decisive—it has developed two different strands: an economic one and a political one. Within the economic ideology that has been dominant since the late 1970s, that is, neoliberalism, a lack of balance has developed between these two dimensions of liberalism. The immediate result is that politics has been pushed into the background, to the point where there really are no alternatives. Herein lies the ideological crisis of democracy.

What, precisely, constitutes this imbalance within liberalism? While *political liberalism* sees the market as a means to the end of ensuring a free and democratic society but concedes an important role to political actors, for *economic liberalism* the market is a pure end in itself. For economic liberalism, free markets and pushback against the state are desirable in and of themselves—and the rest will follow. Efficiency and productivity are the keywords that are repeated again and again as justification, to the point where it seems plausible that whole societies should be organized solely according to economic market principles. Still, despite there seemingly being "no alternatives," there is a lesson that was forgotten and that could be learned from political liberalism and from the reform policies that prevailed at the dawn of the twentieth century: in democracies, this kind of politics must align itself with the interests of the populace, or markets and special interests can undermine it.

We contend that over time the economic philosophy of markets has driven the political ideas of liberalism *ad absurdum.* The primacy of democracy was sacrificed to the seamless operation of market transactions. As a result, politics will have to be reinvented in order to give it more scope and to conceive democracy and certain rights as something other than collateral damage of the markets, namely, as *values in themselves.* In that sense, our book can be understood as an immanent critique of economic liberalism and a plea to return to political liberalism.

Some might argue in response that the ideals of political liberalism, such as equality and democracy, were never fully realized and implemented. Nor is it possible to deny altogether that historically these ideals have often been instrumentalized for the wrong purposes—not least the desire to render societies submissive. Naturally, political liberalism has always been committed to ideas that it never achieved. The founding fathers of the United States were, among other things, fathers, not mothers—and they were slaveholders. Equality, for them, meant the equality of white property owners. When John Stuart Mill and Alexis de Tocqueville were writing their texts, slavery was still widespread. Despite the progressive movements of the late nineteenth century, women's suffrage first came about in the 1910s, and it was only in the 1960s that the civil rights movement achieved actual equal rights for African Americans. Today, structural racism endures, and the social opportunities of men and women remain unequal in both the United States and Europe.[9] For some, therefore, the crisis of democracy is a permanent condition. For these people, it must seem almost cynical to be talking about a crisis only now that white men are also affected. In this sense, the recent focus on "globalization's losers" also lets us forget that globalization has always produced losers—and that Trump and Brexit voters are a very particular brand of losers.

Nevertheless, political liberalism has at least articulated ideals that social movements can pursue. These ideals provided a sounding board that allowed suffragettes, civil rights activists, and other social movements to formulate their own goals in terms of a critique of the discrepancy between political rhetoric and actual practice. In this sense, democracy is a constant search for equality and freedom, not so much their ultimate realization. Such political idealism and political values are necessary in order to denounce reality. And, as we insist, there has to be a balance between economic, political, and civil society forces if democracy is to be possible.

This balance is a question of real politics, but it starts by turning our attention away from pure market thinking. For if, as Wendy Brown has so convincingly argued, all political goals are expressed in the language of economics[10]—if, in other words, political success is measured solely in terms of economic growth and unemployment rates—then it is the market, not political struggle and debate, that decides, and the successes of earlier protests and past emancipation movements turn into Pyrrhic victories. The market veils political debates; it turns them into technical questions that are only about efficiency and are not concerned with what really brings society together. In recent years, economic liberalism, in its neoliberal version, has swallowed up political liberalism along with all demands for political emancipation, which it has transformed into questions of consumption and lifestyle. The origins of today's crisis of democracy lie within liberalism itself. How could this happen, and how can we escape from the horns of this dilemma? This is the focus of our book.

Salvaging Political Liberalism

Under neoliberalism, consumer wishes and identitarian individualism blossomed in unprecedented profusion, while at the same time everything social was allowed to erode. Fare thee well, solidarity! This is a fragile way of organizing societies that can work during a boom. But what happens, under these circumstances, given increasing inequality and spatial separation, when the market's promises of salvation turn out not to be true? When even consumer happiness is no longer certain, given one's own personal indebtedness and stagnating wages? When the responsibility for the problem seems to lie with ourselves? And when, at the same time, "the elites" are stuffing their pockets, and all decisions are being made behind closed doors? Everything seems possible in theory, but alone we are powerless when faced with an increasingly complex society whose workings we no longer understand. The angry citizen is a consequence of this loss of power and authority, which once seemed like individual emancipation. The paralysis of the individual becomes the fury of the masses.

Faced with the debris, one thing suddenly seems clear again: politics must not be left to the demagogues. The critique that already exists must therefore have political consequences—and something with which to oppose the fearmongering and platitudinous sloganeering. The starting point must be an analysis of how we got here. The tendencies toward crisis that we are discussing are not an inescapable cosmic event that has broken in on us from outside. What we are seeing, therefore, is not adequately described as a political swing to the right. The redemptive promise of the neoliberal revolution—individual freedom and self-determination—simply has remained unfulfilled for too many. Societies no longer have a common project; they are reduced to the sum of their individuals. The market and the higher value ascribed to private interests undermine the common good. But where the social reality is shattered, where no shared public good is created, where no narrative of a united society prevails, social cohesion is also endangered. A society that is divided in this way, in which all individuals are thrown back upon themselves, is susceptible to agitators.

The first wave of protests was still broadly anticapitalist—think of the Occupy movement and Podemos—and correspondingly diffuse. The field of battle was clear, but it was hard to get a grip on the enemy. Trump's and the Brexiteers' critique of the elites gave more specific expression to the opposition, with a rightward twist: it is all about winners and losers, the establishment versus the electorate. In the crisis, therefore, the fronts do not necessarily only follow the traditional left-right line of demarcation. Actually, the gulf between opponents and supporters of globalization runs perpendicular to the old right-left division and is often deepened and magnified by the urban-rural divide. Old conflict structures, once considered obsolete in light of modernization, are reconstituted.

In our opinion, the liberal democratic model is now at a turning point. With this, debates from the Enlightenment that had been considered resolved have once again become matters of controversy. Economic liberalism, sharpened to a fine point by the neoliberalism of the past forty years, robbed liberalism's political framework of its value, and now that framework needs to be redrawn.

After tracing the emergence of the politics of no alternatives and seeking to understand the common roots of the transatlantic crisis of liberal democracy in Chapter 2, we will take a look at the differences between Europe and the United States. At the core of dominant U.S. political traditions is a special understanding of the state and its role in the economy and society. Here, belief in the self-correcting powers of the market is especially prominent. Government is seen as a burden and potential threat to freedom and, as such, as something that should be kept small. Chapter 3 is devoted to the specific forms of the crisis in the United States and links it to cultural, political, and economic characteristics. Many tendencies can be observed with particular clarity here, for the division of society into ideological camps and into rich and poor is far more pronounced than in European countries. This part of the book foregrounds the specifically American elements, the "American exceptionalism" of this immanent crisis of liberalism.

That the gap between rich and poor in the United States is unusually deep, and society especially polarized, is reflected not only in the divide between media outlets and gridlock in Congress. In more stable times, the separation of powers serves as a guarantor of American democracy. In a divided country, it only seems to make the rift deeper and to render politics impossible. Moreover, from a historical perspective, inequality has been socially tolerable in the United States. Poverty does not undermine social cohesion as long as individuals can achieve upward mobility through their own efforts. Today, however, the lack of social advancement calls the American dream into question. In view of the extreme inequalities, certain traditions of the political culture seem to have come undone. The promise of social betterment has lost its power as social glue, and the myth of the classless society has become a cynical commentary on a divided nation.

Chapter 4 looks at a comparable structural change that is occurring within European liberalism. There, however, it has unfolded as a double crisis, both at the supranational, European level and at the level of the individual nation-states. In this context, too, we see increasing technocratic dominance and a decoupling of the economy from politics. But the turbulences in the individual E.U. member states are also accompanied by a second, supranational crisis of European democracy. Even more clearly than in the United States, it is a crisis of depoliticization, since the population feels that the institutions of the European Union do not make political sense and experiences them instead as a bureaucratic abomination. There seems to be no foundational identity upon which a common European social project could be constructed. Here too the political idea of a united Europe has been eroded by the economic interests of individual states and markets. Here too economic liberalism has undermined the political idea of Europe and allowed the European Union to atrophy into a mere shell, which lacks those elements that could be identity forming. Every nation-state seems to be its own closest ally. How long will the European Union be able to sustain these tensions before it breaks apart?

The challenges may be daunting. But we also see grounds for hope. In Chapter 5, we take the striving of civil societies as the starting point to reflect on the alternatives to no alternatives. Along with very concrete steps that can be taken at the national level, new thinking about politics is needed—new thinking that is more than merely a step-by-step response to the symptoms. We offer short-term solutions at the national level, where political systems can indeed learn from experiences on the other side of the Atlantic. But solutions on the national level can only go so far. It is time to formulate questions that may also sound utopian, as a means of stimulating thinking about a more political future. What could a new social pact look like, one that can link the conditions for a democratic order with the challenges of a globally integrated economy? What political subject, in the future, could still legitimate political decision-making and thus bring back trust in mechanisms for political decision-making? How, going forward, can the decoupled spaces of politics and the economy be connected in such a way that just distribution and participative opportunities are created? What can we learn from one another across the Atlantic? At the beginning of this development, there needs to be a political debate about these questions and a clearer understanding of the roots of popular unrest.

Chapter 2

Failed Promises and the Logic of Necessity

If it were possible to link individual decades with intellectual trends, the 1990s would be the decade of economic liberalism. Not quite five years after the fall of the Berlin Wall, on July 12, 1994, when President Bill Clinton addressed the population of Berlin for the first time, market thinking seemed unbeatable. Speaking to the fifty thousand people who had assembled on Pariser Platz, across from the Brandenburg Gate—the symbol of Europe's newly won unity and the end of the Cold War—he promised, "America is on your side, now and forever." His speech focused on the liberal market economy as the motor of global integration and simultaneously as the guarantor of freedom. At the climax of his remarks, Clinton interpreted the opening of the Brandenburg Gate as an emblem of the opening of markets and societies. Together, confident and determined, Germany, Europe, and the United States would stride through this gate toward a shared "destiny" of "peace and hope" in a Europe "where free markets and prosperity know no borders."[1] Clinton's closing words were no less triumphal. Nothing, he said, must be allowed to stand in the way of the expansion of markets and democracies in a Europe "united in peace, united in freedom, united in progress for the first time in history. Nothing will stop us. All things are possible."[2]

The exultant tone of the speech is explained by the historical context in which Clinton gave it. In the 1970s, neoliberalism had already begun its global triumphal march in Great Britain and the United States, where the governments, step by step, had handed parts of the public sector over to private business. After the fall of the Iron Curtain, there seemed to be no more political limits to market thinking anywhere else either. Doubts about globalization were brushed aside. Without systemic alternatives, the triumph of the liberal model seemed unstoppable. Whether in Europe, the United States, or on other continents, no matter, the outcome was obvious: externally, free trade would ensure peace and cosmopolitanism among peoples; internally, markets would make ramshackle social systems more efficient and, at the same time, place barriers in the way of excessive state intervention.

In the decades following 1989, this market philosophy quickly spread from Prime Minister Margaret Thatcher and President Ronald Reagan in the Anglophone countries—the core territories of liberal capitalism—to Eastern Europe, where the politics of no alternatives would be tested in shock therapy and made workable for the rest of the world.[3] As the liberal project was being realized, critical voices remained marginal. The dominant idea was that history had arrived at a turning point. Francis Fukuyama gave this thesis its most pointed expression and became known for prophesying the "end of history"—meaning the absolutely unrivaled character of liberal democracy as a social concept with no alternatives.[4] In a world that was more and more closely interwoven, he argued, political integration and the opening up of societies were a necessity and, even more, a blessing. The markets, as the drivers of this change, would—entirely automatically—also ensure political and cultural progress, while putting the ideological battles of human history to rest once and for all.

Today, little seems to remain of Bill Clinton's and Francis Fukuyama's euphoria, which merely exemplifies the dominant spirit of the late twentieth century. The dream of the end of history seems to have burst. At the height of the euphoria, around the millennium, the way forward still seemed clear: the state, a bureaucratic monster of institutionalized inefficiency, needed to be tightened up and slimmed down so as to save public money and leave the distribution of goods to the markets, which were more efficient anyway. The downside of these political decisions can be seen today. Education, environmental protection, construction of infrastructure, social insurance, and health care systems—everything, in other words, that made modern society possible—were hollowed out by market logic as it ran rampant. Entitlement to government support was now based on the willingness to work, and as a consequence, employment became the sole criterion of social participation. How is this supposed to function in a postindustrial society in which there is not enough work for everyone?

As if individual fears of downward mobility and mistrust of elites were not enough, they were supplemented, especially after the attack on the World Trade Center in 2001 and the attacks in Paris in November 2015, by the fear of terrorism. The result was an explosive cocktail that is now being discharged in the form of mass demonstrations and protest votes. Is it surprising that there is resistance to what is often characterized as globalization? Or that there is fear of the external, the other, of competition with poorer countries for work, of the free movement of people and capital? Resistance to the liberal consensus and to the economic and social politics that until now seemed to have no alternative is growing on both sides of the Atlantic in the form of broad oppositional movements. We are experiencing a turn away from the basic assumptions about globalization that Bill Clinton was still able to trumpet two decades ago. The political consensus is breaking down, and the credibility of liberal economic policies is coming in for more and more criticism: the logic of inherent necessity no longer seems compelling when governmental expenditures for social welfare are cut back with the argument that there are no alternatives and coffers are empty, while at the same time banks are being bailed out. How are you supposed to explain that to an unemployed person?

This chapter looks at the structural dynamics of the crisis of liberal democracy, at those developments, in other words, that Europe and the United States have in common. The crisis points well beyond the individual phenomena of Trump, Brexit, or the National Front. To dismiss Trump as an agitator—which he certainly also is—is to ignore the long-term developments that have led to the crisis of democracy. Anyone who makes populism too much the center of their perspective runs the danger of dismissing the protest movements as irrational expressions of a hysterical populace. But the protest, as we shall see, is a reaction to a specific historical development, not a sudden eruption of emotion. The individual contexts that we will describe in the coming chapters only make sense against the backdrop of a shared, long-term crisis. It bears repeating: the populists are only the outgrowths of a more profound crisis, not its cause. Instead, the roots of today's crisis lie in liberalism's failed promises.

The Great Promise

Before economic liberalism, with its apolitical belief in markets, accelerated in the 1970s and led to today's crisis of democracy, there was a long period when political liberalism actually set the tone. Postwar politics, in Europe and the United States, did not seek unchecked liberalization of the markets, but instead aimed to defend society against the power of the private sector in specific political realms. The reforms of the new progressive liberals at the turn of the twentieth century were followed, after the Great Depression of the late 1920s and 1930s, by the creation of modern welfare states and a compromise between the state, capital, and labor. It is important to understand this "Great Promise" of social advancement for the working class if we are to comprehend how it was even possible for Trump and all the other populists to emerge.

In both Europe and the United States, the decades after the end of World War II saw an extraordinary economic boom. Keynesian economic policies reflected Henry Ford's idea of allowing pay increases for his workers as a means of guaranteeing the sales of his Model T. Productivity increases in private industry were distributed among the workers in a fashion that was analogous to the macroeconomic measures being taken by government. Markets were tamed in order to serve broader segments of society. The result, for businesses, was a stability that affected sales and demand: increases in income allowed the growing middle class to afford the automobiles, refrigerators, and television sets that were being produced in the industrial zones of the American Midwest, the French northeast, and the German Ruhr Valley. With this, both private market participants and workers in Western Europe and North America found a compromise that linked mass consumption and mass production, even if it took different forms in the different contexts. As the pie grew, so did the pieces.

Politics and the economy struck a balance, and the actual Great Promise was built on this compromise. Redistribution allowed mass consumption. But this was only one part of the story. In addition, the promise was linked to a particular understanding of citizenship. Citizens, male and female, were seen not merely as economic actors or as voters who would only need to be mobilized at election time, but as social beings who required a certain basic amount of social security in order to be able to participate meaningfully in democracy at all. This concept of *social citizenship*[5] underlay the creation of welfare states in the 1930s and their expansion in the 1960s. With these sorts of security measures in place and in times of national full employment, everyone, at least in theory, enjoyed the possibility of doing better. Upward mobility was further enabled by publicly funded educational systems that allowed (almost) free access to school and university, and thus brought the hope of a better life concretely within reach. At the same time, social security systems decoupled work in the market economy from the stresses of the struggle for survival. Investments in public infrastructure were made with similar objectives in mind.

Expressed in the language of liberalism, in the post–World War II era, the individual was no longer seen exclusively as a benefit-maximizing *homo economicus* but rather as a citizen, a person who would attain full majority based on universal basic security. This promise of social mobility was the social glue that today has become brittle. The shared education, a concept of shared citizenship, and assembled social benefits that flowed from belonging to the nation allowed broad segments of society to live in relative economic security. These institutions of the Fordist era also created a commonwealth that generated a sense of togetherness. Organs of the media—then mostly government funded—were not the least important contributors to this communal sense. By presenting a unified version of reality, they were far from the splintering of reality that we experience now, in the light of fake news, polarized television shows, and social media.

This Great Promise also had a significant spatial dimension. For one thing, naturally, industrial regions blossomed as more and more workers advanced into the middle class and adopted corresponding goals and lifestyles. For another thing, this new, rising middle class built new housing developments and, thanks to the cross-subsidization of public infrastructure, could also afford to live in more distant neighborhoods. In the United States, in the years following World War II, this led to the expansion of suburbs, where (above all) white middle-class residents looked for, and found, their green idyll.

Europe had its own wonders as alternatives to the American Dream: the *trente glorieuses*—a thirty years' boom—in France and the *Wirtschaftswunder*, or economic miracle, in Germany. While they may not have been implemented to the extent of the American Levittowns and hypersuburbanization, row houses and single-family homes outside the inner city soon came to represent the dream of a mass utopia for Europeans, too.

Meanwhile, on the world stage, the clash between contrasting social and political systems gave further emphasis to this evolution of the welfare state and social citizenship and, as such, to national unity. In contrast to the Soviet Union, Western welfare states were meant to demonstrate the advantages of capitalism as an alternative that was envisioned as the foil to "actually existing socialism." In light of the institutions of Fordism, the Keynesian economic orientation, and its redistributive macroeconomic approach, capitalism seemed to have rounded off its sharp edges and tamed its business cycles. A utopia come true?

It should be noted that the golden age of Fordism was never quite as golden as it may seem from today's perspective.[6] Nostalgia for the industrial jobs of Fordism, for such public goods as education and infrastructure, is considerable today, given the contemporary situation. But workers had to be lured to their repetitive and often stupefying jobs on the assembly lines with promises and threats. More important, especially as seen from today's vantage point, in the 1950s and 1960s, not everyone shared equally in the success of Western societies—quite apart from the fact that these successes were achieved at the expense of other populations in other parts of the world.[7] In the United States, it was above all the white workers in the processing industries of the Northeast and Midwest (the same groups who gave Trump his electoral victory in 2016), who benefited from Fordism.[8] In Europe, too, women and minorities long remained excluded from the Great Promise—and remain so today to some extent. On capitalism's sunny side, they were allocated only seats in the shade.

And yet, at least in theory, the promise seemed to apply to everyone. One could even argue that the rise of the women's movement and the civil rights movement in the 1960s and 1970s were first enabled by Fordism, which made it possible to even think about expanding political and economic participation and opening it up to the whole of society. This hope of emancipation, which was never actually fulfilled, translated into political engagement and demands for progressive reforms, reforms that would be shared by all—until they were not.

The Crisis as Countermovement

Interestingly, it is not the immediate losers of globalization who chose Trumpism in its various national variants. It is those who feared losing their socioeconomic status—the people who, before the politics of no alternatives, profited from the political-economic arrangement or, more specifically, from the Great Promise of the postwar period we have just described. Trumpism needs to be understood as part of a broader countermovement that extends beyond individual national contexts, because the Fordist working classes are "no longer winning."[9] The beneficiaries of that era are today's protest voters among downwardly mobile society. At least since the 1970s, it is not only the hopes of marginalized groups but those of the recently successful that have been massively jolted.

The national and social compromise among employers, workers, and government itself, which had emerged in the years following World War II, was tossed overboard. The Keynesian-Fordist order based on social mobility and gradually equalizing class relations collapsed. Competitiveness in the global markets—no longer redistribution—became the all-important criterion for decision-making.

It was the government, to be sure, that first made all this possible through its massive contributions to the reduction of transport and communications costs and thus to the expansion of international trade. Starting with the United States, almost all governments played an active part in the establishment of a global infrastructure for the distribution of goods. Thus, governments financed the construction of container ports, the dredging of rivers, the deepening of harbors, and the raising of bridges—all for the benefit of the global market and globally active firms. To break up the oligopolies in transport, governments also deregulated transport and communication chains.[10] The social and ecological costs associated with the transport of goods and people were externalized. Here, the United States was in the vanguard, but other countries followed America's lead, partly in order to remain competitive in the global economy. Today the question must be asked, was this just?

The lower transportation and communication costs, for their part, brought the working classes of Fordism into competition with nonregulated workers in other places and thus into enormous distress and financial difficulties. Unions forfeited organizational capacity and negotiating flexibility and gradually also lost their relevance. It is not just that the work disappeared that, until the 1970s, had been accompanied by rising incomes. Nor was it only that factories closed and whole regions were depopulated as a result of deindustrialization. At the same time that these deep structural changes took place the channels for advancement were shutting down, above all in education. This was especially pronounced in the United States. In the 1970s, tuition at private universities such as Harvard exploded. Even at public universities, tuition fees were gradually introduced. The more society was being transformed into a postindustrial knowledge society—in other words, the more important educational certification was becoming for advancement—the more difficult it also became to afford the corresponding degrees. That the cost of college has meanwhile reached dizzying heights and that many of Bernie Sanders's supporters were heavily indebted college students and recent graduates are therefore not very surprising.

While the industrial cities of the postwar era gradually evolved into postindustrial cities of the service sector, a new success narrative unfolded. In knowledge societies, everybody would be able to benefit from the sustainable and creative work opportunities afforded by the New Economy. It was just a matter of acquiring the right skills. The critique of Fordism's rigidity could now unfold to its full extent. Deregulation and flexibilization were introduced in other spheres of life as well and became goals to strive for even in people's personal lives. All this was according to a *new* Great Promise—the promise of the efficiency of markets. Efficient markets would correspond to the differentiation and multiplicity of postindustrial societies. Finally, it would be possible to put an end to the discriminatory practices of postwar governments. Tolerance and multiculturalism became slogans of this social trend, which gave wings to existing social movements in Europe and the United States but also began to diffuse political activism and foreground individual questions of self-fulfillment and identity.[11]

The Best of All Possible Worlds

As the Fordist compromise came undone, the new promise centered on market efficiency to deliver the best of all possible worlds: a vision of meritocracy where the discriminations of the Fordist era could be overcome and individual self-fulfilment was a possibility for all.

The pivotal idea of market-driven emancipation was already gathering speed during the 1930s, in other words, well before the neoliberal revolution of the 1970s. At that time, thinkers already began to reconceive liberal society as an alternative to the totalitarian state. The idea developed of the market as a bulwark against the state, whose centralized power was seen by increasing numbers of commentators as having been the source of the Third Reich and the rise of fascist regimes. Austrian economist Friedrich von Hayek, in particular, argued that planned economies and state centralization lead to tyranny, in other words, that state intervention in markets necessarily limits individual freedom and hence poses a danger for democracy. Markets, on the other hand, were presented as the only free and democratic way to organize modern societies, with their complex division of labor.[12]

Notably, when von Hayek wrote this, it interested no one. The Fordist welfare state was under way, and politics enjoyed greater prominence than economics. At first, therefore, von Hayek's work remained a marginal opinion, which would attract notice only much later. Not until the 1970s, when the era of Keynesian Fordism had entered its final stage, signaled by the end of the Bretton Woods agreement and the oil crises of the Organization of the Petroleum-Exporting Countries (OPEC), did people pull von Hayek's theories out of the drawer where they had been languishing. In 1973, when the Bretton Woods system, which had stabilized the international political economy of the postwar period, collapsed, and in the following years, when two oil crises led to considerable shocks within national economies, including "stagflation" (high inflation accompanied by simultaneously high unemployment) in the United States, Keynesianism seemed to have no more answers left to give when it came to explaining and managing crises. At the same time, technological innovations were beginning to undermine and delegitimize the Fordist compromise. Containerization and computerization created infrastructures for the globalization of production networks and thus for the integration of national markets into a global market. It was possible to organize supply chains across enormous distances and to move the sites of extraction and production to low-wage countries.[13]

After the end of Fordism in the 1970s, the market suddenly appeared as a means to end the crisis and defend society against an all-powerful state. In 1974, von Hayek received the Nobel Prize in Economics for his work on the market as a medium of information. Two years later, the prize went to Milton Friedman, Ronald Reagan's favorite economist, who, with his influence on Chile's economic policy—the laboratory of neoliberalism—had a lasting effect not just on academic debates but on political practice as well.[14] The belief that markets fundamentally deliver a more efficient allocation of goods became the credo of developing neoliberalism. Governments, it seemed, no longer had the capacity to come up with an overview of modern economies in their complexity. Hence, they could not steer them centrally either. And even if they could, their intervention would inevitably and severely distort the market signals and upset the balance among them.

In addition, more and more emphasis was placed on the view that public officials, just like private individuals, would act in their own interest, not that of the public. Actual political decision making regarding the production and availability of specific goods was thus transferred from the state bureaucracy to the market.[15] Ultimately, as Friedman argued in the historical context of America's 1960s racial conflicts, this was also a good thing because markets were color-blind and hence fundamentally progressive when it came to politics.[16] The promise of individual liberation seemed to cater to the zeitgeist of the civil rights and student movements, but hollowed out more collectivist visions of social progress.

In short, markets should be the judges and organizing mechanisms of social development, for they were considered more democratic and flexible and would do away with overly rigid state bureaucracies. The story of the rise of neoliberalism and the reemergence of market thinking has been told many times over. We know how it became socially acceptable after the crises of the mid-1970s—how first transport and communications, then financial markets and social welfare systems, and finally the military and public education were privatized and deregulated, and how the market doctrine spread throughout the world in myriad countries, assuming country-specific forms. While we do not want to tell this story again, we would simply like to point out that with this sudden reversal of political liberalism, economic liberalism came to dominate the discourse and with it the assumption that politics and governmental action had become superfluous. If the 1970s saw Fordist Keynesianism enter its terminal crisis, the 1990s constituted the historical moment when its underlying principles were fully abandoned.

Practical Necessities of the Third Way

In light of the supposed lack of a systemic alternative after the fall of the Berlin Wall, various administrations on both sides of the Atlantic—for example, Bill Clinton in the United States, Tony Blair in Great Britain, and, later, Gerhard Schröder in Germany—tried to come up with a political consensus that would be capable of attracting the support of the majority, especially those people at the center of their societies. The political slogan for this consensus was pragmatism. The idea was to end ideological trench warfare—something that even seemed possible in light of the failure of the Soviet Union. The ideology of socialism appeared to have lost its power and its political practice to have run aground. No longer was there any need to convince those constituents with a soft spot for socialism of the advantages of liberal capitalism through pension schemes and other security systems.

Thus, the center-left parties in Europe and the United States moved to the right in their economic and social policies. This politics became known as the Third Way. The battle between the ideologies of socialism and capitalism seemed to have been decided, a final compromise found. The Third Way became a popular slogan that was used to denote precisely this middle-of-the road, supra-party, postideological pragmatism. In many countries, despite lip service to social democracy, this consensus was oriented to neoliberal market politics. It offered an alternative for everyone. To pursue the Third Way was to attempt to actually *create* the best of all possible worlds: a world without alternatives.

For two decades, this liberalism of the center looked like the royal road. It promised much to many, and indeed seemed to offer something for everybody, thus making it possible to appeal to broad majorities. If economic liberalism and its logic of efficiency appealed to the conservative camps among voters, progressives could emphasize its multiculturalism and normative values. The move to the right may have left a bitter aftertaste among the left wings within some parties on both sides of the Atlantic. The response was to compromise with them by introducing open identity politics. The theory of reflexive modernization, as developed by its proponents Ulrich Beck and Anthony Giddens, played an important role here, as it lent the narrative of globalization and its imperatives an identitarian political dimension.[17] Open markets and free societies, so the credo went, were naturally symbiotic. In this way, in the late twentieth century, the economic dimension of liberalism (expansion of markets) and its political dimension (the values of cosmopolitanism and national and global solidarity) seemed perfectly married. This meant, however, that the actually political questions were shoved into the background.

It would be wrong to present the inevitability and promise of salvation by the markets as the only characteristic of the Third Way, although these features were especially pronounced there. Bill Clinton's proglobalization policy is strongly reminiscent of the logic of earlier forms of liberalism, which were no less convinced that the welfare of society was bound up with the liberalization of markets. But what seems entirely new in the context of the last decades is the idea of a lack of alternatives to particular policies, accompanied by the full-blown depoliticization of the state and its future. Adam Smith, the father of modern liberalism, spent an entire book detailing specific basic tasks of the state, such as national defense, the funding of the justice system, and the building of infrastructure. Even Milton Friedman, the figurehead of neoliberalism, assigned the state a certain role in educational policy and social welfare. But under the Third Way, the state has been conceived as a hindrance per se, as something that is inferior to the market in nearly all respects.

With reference to historical necessity and buttressed by the end of the Cold War and the downfall of really existing forms of socialist state formation, both ends of the political spectrum thus came to believe that only one form of economic and political organization made sense. The end of history and the perceived lack of system alternatives seemed to render superfluous any debate over types of politics. Because globalization was supposedly both inevitable and fundamentally desirable, there was necessarily only one way to deal with it. Thus, Margaret Thatcher talked about TINA ("There Is No Alternative"), and Angela Merkel, some three decades after her, spoke of the lack of any alternative (*Alternativlosigkeit*).

The End of the Nation-State?

This logic of practical necessity had a politically instrumental dimension: politicians could point to it as a way to realize political projects that were unpopular in liberal

democracies, such as cuts to social and health care benefits or the privatization of education. Under the banner of
efficiency and individual freedom, public goods became
new territories to be conquered by the private sector. This
groupthink sought the well-being of society exclusively in
the opening and expansion of markets, and linked this project—which was strongly normative, although outwardly it
often appeared to be entirely neutral and technical—with
the vision of a cosmopolitan, open society. Adherents of
this view were also able to link it to existing traditions of
liberal thought. Not only were there no alternatives: globalization itself was inevitable and was accompanied by consequences that quite simply made a certain brand of politics
necessary, as we have seen, for the benefit of all.

At its core, the idea that there are no alternatives is
based on the assumption that the forces of globalization,
the markets, are something separate and distinct from
society. Since markets have been deemed external, multi-
national, and indeed global, it often seems that local and
national politicians have little influence over them. This
logic seems almost self-evident today and has even found
its way into everyday language, for example, when we talk
about the "reaction of the markets" or about a given event
that could set off "turbulence in the economy."[18] In light of
these external forces, if the government, minimally, wants
to secure resources and ensure prosperity in its competition with other nation-states, it can only position itself
in accordance with market logic. Therefore, it must get
rid of slack, think more entrepreneurially, and become
more competitive by reducing its budgets. Abjuring direct
intervention, this argument narrows the space for political action to the creation of incentives for private actors.

Government, accordingly, should stay out of any affairs that have to do with markets, since government is less efficient, and, as von Hayek pointed out, even its most minor intervention distorts the market's functioning.

Yielding to these arguments, liberal and social democratic parties on both sides of the Atlantic have mostly abandoned the idea that there is a role for governments in globalization—much less one that would be emancipatory! Kenichi Ohmae offered the most pointed formulation of this erroneous perspective in 1995, when he prophesied the end of the nation-state, further developing Fukuyama's thesis of the end of history.[19] Ohmae's core claim—namely, that in the course of globalization nation-states would lose more and more influence and power—has meanwhile become the mantra of social scientists, politicians, international institutions, and public intellectuals. But this belief is not only misleading, which it certainly is; it is also dangerous.

The theory that the nation-state is disappearing is false because it contradicts the facts, even if the normative cosmopolitan impulse on which it is based is understandable. Without national governments, globalization is not possible. These political institutions are necessary to secure property rights, make contracts enforceable, provide public goods, stabilize currencies, and so on. The free market, it turns out, is a utopia that cannot exist by relying entirely on itself. Globalization, as the increased mobility of goods, people, capital, and information, was dependent on the state when it first emerged, and it remains dependent on it now. From the creation of abstract national economies, to the expansion of markets across national and continental borders, to exchange via global production networks, the nation-state was and remains the central actor in international political economy.[20]

But the work that national governments do for globalization often goes unnoticed, hidden in the technical details. This work, alongside market-creating mechanisms such as the negotiation of free trade agreements, includes the nonregulation of certain markets—in logistics, for example—in order to enable mobility in international markets. In addition, there are investments in research and development, education, and infrastructure, or, fundamentally, the stabilization of currencies and the maintenance of law and order, which can only be provided by the state, not the market.[21] Not least, there are also the tasks of rescuing banks and intervening in cases when markets fail.

Where Roads Diverge

As states seemingly disappeared and liberal progressives on both sides of the Atlantic surrendered to the logics of practical necessity, the middle class stagnated, if it did not actually lose ground. The stealthy process of deregulation and privatization of public goods had been tolerable for many, since it only gradually attracted notice. With the financial crisis, however, a more or less cautious optimism gave way, once and for all, to lasting doubt and skepticism. The formerly industrial middle class's fears of a loss of social and economic status were now joined by a lack of prospects for moving up. For large segments of the population, the American dream has burst, and the European miracles of the postwar period have lost their magic. The ideal of middle-class life has been unmasked as a political myth lacking any foundation in reality.

Many people also feel left behind in a very physical sense. Numerous countries postponed the financing of public works. Germany's physical infrastructure may still be in relatively good shape, but reliance on public-private partnerships has meant, even there, that the private sector has gained access to the construction of public projects. In the case of railroads, for example, profitability concerns have led to the shutting down of less traveled routes. This "bypass" logic, which also affects other kinds of infrastructure (internet, highways, and so on), runs along the existing fault lines between urban and rural areas, rich and poor. Instead of a logic that would have made public means available to sustain social cohesion and mobility, cross-subsidization between unequal population groups was sacrificed to the rationale of increasing efficiency. In the United States, this phenomenon is sometimes called spatial mismatch. People live too far away from potential workplaces, with the result that inequality is reproduced based on spatial and institutional conditions.

This spatial incongruence seems to have become a mass phenomenon and is closely linked with the geography of those people who have been left behind. This can also be observed in relation to Trump, Brexit, and other forms of populism. A study has shown that the same areas that were decoupled from railroads and other infrastructure disproportionately voted for right-wing nationalists, on both sides of the Atlantic.[22] Pro-Brexit voters, above all, were people who live outside London—the capital of finance—in formerly industrial and coal-mining districts.[23] In the United States, Trump won in areas that were previously bastions of the Democratic Party: the industrial zones of the Midwest near the Great Lakes—the heartland of Fordism—that were deindustrialized and are scornfully referred to as the Rust Belt. Suburbs, too, where the white middle class once longed to live, have lost their luster, with these populations voting broadly for Trump.[24] In France, a very similar picture has emerged. Supporters of the extreme right-wing National Rally live mainly in the northeast, the former industrial region, and in the south, where structural weakness is accompanied by a long and stubborn political tradition of xenophobia. And, in Germany, it is no accident that the Alternative for Germany finds its strongest support in the regions of the country with the greatest structural weakness.

The decoupled regions once stood as symbols for the advancement of (white) workers into the middle class. When the workers' parties, such as the Democrats in the United States or the Social Democrats in Germany, decided to embark on the Third Way and to follow the dictates of the global market, it should actually have been predictable that the one-time workers might turn away and that, based on the spatial propinquity of these groups of voters and the hollowing out of their infrastructures, there could be political consequences. Actually, it is much more surprising that this did not happen a good deal earlier. But traditions appear strong, especially when change occurs gradually, over decades. The decisive moment for the break and the turn away from the status quo only came with the financial crisis of 2008—and the political response to it.

Markets are not always beneficial for society. The claim that they are has always been an argument that served specific historical purposes and special interests. Arguing on the basis of practical necessity and a lack of alternatives comes at a price, however: to many people, politics appears arbitrary and politicians interchangeable. Simplistic belief in markets has undermined the politics of openness and integration. Over the last four decades, the economization of all aspects of life has undermined democracies, while the expansion of markets into all political fields has eroded the political pillars on which European and North American societies were built. This, not populism, is the real essence of the crisis of democracy.

At its heart, therefore, the crisis is a crisis of depoliticization. The inequalities that have escalated as a result of the privatization and deregulation of various goods have turned politics into a sideshow when it comes to societal development. Politicians appear as enablers of the economy; their political party affiliation does not matter. As long as the social glue holds, in other words, as long as everyone senses a personal chance to do better, the market project of liberalizing and privatizing all aspects of life can succeed. Inequalities are accepted with more or less gnashing of teeth as long as there is at least the hope that one's personal pursuit of happiness might succeed. There may be a democratic deficit, which, in fact, has been discussed at length in many quarters since the 1990s. But who cares about the decoupling of elites when, after all, it is happening only gradually and imperceptibly—and there is the possibility that one might soon be part of an elite group oneself?

What happens, though, when suddenly these possibilities for advancement and individual self-fulfillment appear to be blocked for large segments of the population; when the mechanisms that have made this way of life possible no longer work; when the government has no more alternatives to offer, since it no longer can; and when, then, government assistance turns out to be possible after all, if it is the banks that are failing? The fuse is not only set; it is shooting sparks. The lack of alternatives is no longer politically tolerable. Demagogues appear on the scene to offer alternatives. The consensus breaks down.

Politics Roars Back

Of course, Trumpism and Brexit are also nationalistic. Trump flirted with the ultra-right and even gave their agitators prominent roles in the first year of his administration, in the persons of Stephen Bannon and Sebastian Gorka. The fact that, in the run-up to the election, Trump did not distance himself from former Ku Klux Klan leader David Duke spoke volumes about Trump's willingness to play with fire, as did his media-savvy, well-placed, and exaggerated images of foreign and domestic threats, which stoked fears of social decline. But it is not just the xenophobic dimension of nationalism that seems to appeal to many people. Nationalism, apart from the exclusion of outsiders, also holds an emancipatory promise for some non-right-wing Trump supporters, namely, the promise of the nation as a community of solidarity in social and economic matters. Trump understood this, and he was one of the first to know how to turn the failure of the Third Way into political capital.[25]

Crucially, global Trumpism is a countermovement. What we are seeing is the repoliticization of a market thinking that went unquestioned for decades. But this is not a return to the political ideals of liberalism, such as we saw in earlier periods. Instead, it is a nationalist reaction with ultra-right elements. For today's countermovement, what is central is the turn away from the market and from everything that is seen as connected to globalization. During his campaign, Trump made clear that economic liberalism and the weakening of national governments were not in the interest of everyone. He concluded that what was needed was a new, protectionist economic policy, and he insisted on the need to exit from free-trade agreements or at least to renegotiate them. To this were added his demand for reindustrialization of the United States, by means of punitive tariffs on foreign firms, and an infrastructure policy that at first blush looked neo-Keynesian. All this was diametrically opposed to the political consensus of the last forty years and the "business as usual" approach of the Third Way, which had continued even after the financial crisis.

Getting manufacturing companies to come back has become the symbol of a nostalgia stimulated by economic decline. It is not for nothing that references abound to the postwar period and the national compromise between labor and capital, and that they flirt with a longing for a time when jobs were not yet flexibilized and there were careers that brought lifelong security. That, when it comes to decisive issues, this flirtation with Fordism does not amount to a return to the welfare state of the 1950s and 1960s should be clear, however—quite irrespective of whether such a thing would even be possible. Trump's social vision, like that of the Alternative for Germany, the National Rally, and the Brexiteers, contains no notion of social citizenship such as the one that was still at the core of Fordism. There is no talk of restoring such public goods as education, minimum wage, and so on as rights of citizens. On the contrary, based on Trump's early actions as president, the actual direction of his administration's march seems to be toward the further privatization of social goods, accompanied by simultaneous expansion of the repressive organs of government and militarization of the police. The declarations of solidarity expressed in campaign slogans, such as the electoral pronouncements of the National Rally, the Alternative for Germany, and the Brexiteers, were already sounding like empty promises before Trump had taken office—to say nothing of what came after.

Today, despite all the crises of neoliberalism, the argument derived from economic liberalism remains as powerful as it is because it makes a virtue out of a necessity. Not only does it have a negative view of government, which is supposed to hold back and in any case can do nothing about external markets and technological change. It also positively affirms the market and argues in favor of excluding government and politics on the grounds that the globalization of markets is not only inevitable; it is fundamentally positive. In this respect, the arguments of economic liberals coincide with the economic explanation of neoliberal apologists: open markets and their expansion into all realms of life should be welcomed because they quite naturally result in economic exchange and thus in political openness, tolerance, and cosmopolitanism as well. It is this construct of the best of all possible worlds that we need to grapple with in the context of the crisis of democracy, because it ignores the fact that a political counterweight is necessary if liberalism is not to stumble.

At the risk of belaboring the point, politics remains decisive, even if it seems ever more technocratic and nontransparent. The hope of keeping government small is and was a normative one. Government may be more or less visible and may act more indirectly, it is true, but its significance has never been diminished. Government never went away. It could not. But making it seem small and harping on its reduction made it possible to subvert political questions and present them as purely technical detail work. The question is whether and for whose benefit politics is employed. The perception that the state is disappearing is perilous because, with it, the responsiveness of political institutions is reduced. If we do not know that globalization and markets are made by governments, we cannot articulate a critique or make demands for legitimacy and social justice. Protest remains disoriented and can be misused by demagogues and agitators for their own purposes. This is a core problem for the left but one that no longer seems to bother the nationalist right.

The politics of no alternatives is an oxymoron, for the lack of alternatives excludes politics altogether. Politics means autonomous action and free choice among different options, even if the choices that are made are not without consequences. Thus, depoliticization necessarily had to come up against its limit. After the fall of the Berlin Wall, the expansion of markets was still supported and legitimized by pleas for cosmopolitan openness, tolerance, and multiculturalism. These values and normative goals have always served, in the practice of neoliberalism, as the unquestioned foundation of the good expansion of markets, as seen in Bill Clinton's speech.[26] Now, with the collapse of economic liberalism's dogmas, its political legitimation is also called into question. Cosmopolitanism becomes collateral damage of market thinking. Because political goals were always only economically legitimated, we even seem to lack the language to argue in favor of

Democracy in America

Since 2006, the *Economist*, drawing on the research of its Intelligence Unit, has published a ranking of democratic countries worldwide.[1] The report distinguishes four categories: full democracies, flawed democracies, hybrid regimes, and authoritarian regimes. In all the previous rankings, the United States could be found under the rubric of full democracies. But in the ranking for the year 2016, this was no longer the case. For the first time, the United States appeared as a flawed democracy. Is the first democratic country in human history, then, no longer a democratic showplace?

The main reason for the downgrading of the United States may be found in the fact that America's citizens have lost trust in their government, elected representatives, and political parties. This loss of trust did not begin with Donald Trump. It is a long-term process, and Trump's election victory in 2016 represents the temporary culmination of a crisis that began some time ago. If citizens no longer trust their political representatives, then the central pillar of representative democracies begins to wobble and threatens to pull down the whole complex edifice of political legitimacy. No wonder, at such moments as these, that populist movements and actors can effectively mobilize with their slogans, in Europe and also in the United States.

The extent of the current political legitimation crisis in the United States can be gleaned from a survey by the Pew Research Center.[2] Only every fifth American citizen still has confidence in the work of his or her elected representatives—the lowest rating in more than fifty years. Even in the late 1960s, when this question became part of the standard repertoire of opinion research, three out of four respondents expressed their trust in the government. In the interim, almost every second American has become convinced that every individual in the United States would do a better job than the elected politicians. Trust and support surely look different from this.

But what exactly is the source of this mistrust? Where does the gap come from that has opened up between the political elites and those who feel left behind by social and economic developments? It is not just Trump supporters among the marginalized and forgotten, whom Hillary Clinton during the 2016 election campaign notoriously labeled as "deplorable," who have turned away. Broad segments of the middle class and the traditional working class, in particular, have moved far away from the political elite when it comes to their norms and conceptions of value. They long for a new group of politicians who take their fears seriously and are capable of formulating an alternative to the established politics.

The politics of no alternatives, which we have identified as the chief cause of the current crisis of democracy, fell on especially fertile soil in the United States. The crisis has come so far that Trump, with his antiglobalization and partially right-wing populist agenda, was able to mobilize effectively. Meanwhile, those disappointed by the failed promises of economic liberalism stayed away from the voting booth and as a result Trump actually managed to move into the Oval Office.

Many of Trump's voters were surprised by his victory, but the hope and desire of citizens for thoroughgoing political change and for a new political direction that would be better aligned with the interests of broad segments of the population had already been the foundation of Obama's electoral victory in 2008. "Hope" and "change we can believe in" were the slogans Obama wielded so successfully to mobilize the populace during his campaign. At the time, the electoral victory of the first black president was still interpreted as a progressive advance by a society that was continuing to become more democratic. From the vantage point of today and in light of Trump's victory, the 2008 results can also be interpreted differently.

The change Obama promised failed to materialize for many people. There were a few cosmetic amendments and revisions to the politics of no alternatives, but after the financial crisis, which fell in the middle of the 2008 campaign and would eventually cost many citizens their job, their home, and their savings, large parts of the population felt that the impression had been confirmed: the people on top only do politics for the rich, while the interests of the little people play no role at all. Trump's slogan "America First" resonated especially strongly with those who had been excluded from the economic development of recent decades. They were dissatisfied with the growing inequality in the distribution of income and wealth, and they saw few if any opportunities for social betterment for themselves and especially for their children.

In the United States, education, as one of the central transmission belts of social mobility, has become a barely affordable good even for the middle class. Many people realize that their children will one day be worse off than they themselves are. At the same time, however, the politicians and lobbyists, owners and investors who fueled the crisis, because they had irresponsibly and selfishly taken advantage of the latitude that the government with its neoliberal politics of economic deregulation had opened up for them, recovered quickly. After the crisis, they found themselves in circumstances that were at least as good, if not better, than before.

But Trump's electoral victory was not based only on his "America First" agenda. He presented himself effectively as a political outsider, someone not dependent on big money—since he is a multibillionaire himself—and as someone who could formulate and push through a politics that would be in the interest of the forgotten and marginalized. He even kept his distance from the party he was actually running for: after all, the Republicans were also part of the political establishment. And he characterized almost all the media as the enemy, especially, of course, the liberal mainstream media, which was just as much a part of the swamp in Washington as the representatives of big money. The military-industrial complex, from the era of the Cold War, seems to have been replaced in the collective imagination of many U.S. citizens by a media-money complex.

American Exceptionalism

The question remains why, precisely in the United States, the country with exemplary democratic traditions, has the crisis of the model of liberal democracy assumed such a manifest form? Why have the the consequences of globalization had such an untrammeled impact on its social and economic situation? A few became obscenely rich, while the majority remained excluded from the growing economic prosperity. Why were the forces of right-wing populism able to mobilize so effectively in the United States, a country where, historically, populism was mostly progressive and came from the left? Why has the same democracy that, as the first new nation, has been celebrated as a kind of blueprint for a democratic order now been the hardest hit by the legitimation crisis?

In short, what are the reasons the crisis of democracy has taken such a radical turn in the United States? Since we define the crisis as a global one, it must be possible to uncover the reasons for the specific forms it has assumed in this instance. Here, neoliberalism encountered a liberal market economy with historically pronounced features. For a long time, this was not a big problem. On the contrary, in the political culture and the idea of "American exceptionalism," we can observe many of the elements that also make up neoliberalism.[3] In a certain sense, neoliberalism can even be called an American invention. For the people of the United States, the market played a central role in its national mythology from the outset. Government, here, was only meant to be supportive. Certainly it should never intervene too strongly: this was the only way the productive forces of capitalism would be able to unfold. It all worked, too, as long as the market was able to fulfill the promises of growth and social mobility. But when this does not work, the United States is not well positioned. So, what precisely makes the U.S. crisis specific?

First, in comparison to many European countries, the United States lacks the necessary political means and legitimation that would allow the government to intervene in the market and give its people, irrespective of market developments, the resources they need to be active citizens. Thus, American citizens' norms and ideas about their country open the door wide to neoliberal policies, as we have seen in recent years. But the same norms and ideas also result in a peculiar institutional structure, which functions as long as the market is able to fulfill its promises. When this does not happen, the impact of the crisis is all the more powerful. This is the *cultural* dimension of the current predicament.

Second, the crisis is an *economic* one, as demonstrated by developments in the labor market and the drastically increased inequality in income and wealth. The core founding myth of the United States is of a historically unique nation characterized by pronounced individualism and a strong belief in market mechanisms and small government. But this arrangement can only work socially if there is a sense of community that extends beyond special interests— something that under circumstances of inequality seems to be less and less the case. Here, the financial and economic crisis of 2008 served as a catalyst. It intensified the structural weaknesses of the liberal market economy and allowed economic inequality to reach an almost unbearable level.

Third, in recent years, America's economic inequalities have increasingly translated into *political* ones. Money has become ever more important in politics. As a result, the system of checks and balances that the founding fathers so prudently installed as a means of preventing the abuse of politics in the interest of a small ruling class has degenerated into a system of permanent blockade and stasis. Built into the DNA of the political system, the division of power had been supposed to prevent the excessive concentration of administrative capacity in the hands of the few and in this way to protect democracy. But in periods of growing polarization and increasing economic inequality, these control mechanisms have been developed *ad absurdum*. What was once designed to enable and protect democracy became a danger for it. The refusal on both sides to make political compromises has led to a loss of legitimacy among the population—and to the desire for authentic outsiders, which Trump satisfied.

These three different dimensions of the crisis of democracy in the United States—cultural, economic, and political—are closely interconnected and render the fundamental, immanent crisis of liberalism more acute. John Locke is reputed to have said that Americans were "born free," and Alexis de Tocqueville agreed with him. This freedom of the individual—a political myth that is especially powerful in the United States—also fueled the neoliberal project. In the last few years, its cost for American society has multiplied.

Culture Matters: The Ideas Behind the Crisis

American citizens' mistrust of their national government is part and parcel of the idea of American exceptionalism. The myth of the United States is expressed as a tension between national self-aggrandizement, as reflected in the notion of "American exceptionalism," on the one hand, and an almost completely contradictory critical distancing from the state as an abstract idea, on the other. Alexis de Tocqueville pointed to this crucial difference between the United States and Europe, and many other social scientists after him have done the same. In years past, these writers still emphasized the superiority of American democracy, which they saw precisely in its wariness toward central government. Nowadays, however, the basic conditions that allowed democracy's unique functioning in the United States seem to have only limited applicability. The presumed cultural predisposition of a supposedly healthy mistrust of government is no longer in itself the unique selling point of an especially vigilant democracy. Instead, it has developed into a concrete and pathological problem that confronts the present.

In the national mythology of the United States, the individual takes center stage. Naturally, it would be hard to derive a feeling of community solely from an idea of this kind. And while the market does play an important role in social integration, it also does not produce emotional glue that is necessary to give citizens a sense of national belonging. Likewise, the national myth of "American exceptionalism" offers only rudimentary notions of how an ideal state or an ideal human condition can or should be created by social planning. The dominant images are of a condition of striving and becoming and of the experience of an unconstrained life. Notions of individual freedom, social mobility, and pragmatism define national imaginaries. So in the United States a complex mix of theological and secular assumptions was assembled from which individuals could derive a collective identity. It is this specific relationship among citizens, the government, and the market that makes it possible to explain the particular features of the crisis in the United States.

Tocqueville already noted that the pursuit of happiness served as an anchor point for the commonwealth. This notion and others like it are so deeply engrained in America's national self-concept that Tocqueville's observations of a primarily rural, Protestant, and Anglo-Saxon populace remain valid even for an urbanized, (post)industrial, and multicultural society in the twenty-first century. But it was also Tocqueville who noted that this separate striving of individuals could represent a danger for democracy, for the elevation of the individual requires some common denominator as its counterweight. If the latter is lacking, society is in danger of breaking down into its individual parts.

To explain why individualism plays such an important role in the United States, especially as compared to Europe, scholars frequently point out that for arriving immigrants, the new nation offered the possibility of escape from the social, political, and economic dead ends of their lives in Europe. Liberated from Europe's class structures, the immigrants could begin new, free, self-determined lives on the North American continent—or at least some of them could.

The idea of the individual pursuit of happiness and success also shaped the mythology of westward expansion, all the way to the Pacific coast. The notion of the "frontier," as the boundary between wilderness and civilization, may have been an "exit option," but it also offered the hope of a better world, one that could lend meaning to an individual's actions. On one hand, it made it possible to escape from authority; on the other, the wilderness also offered the option of creating something new.

Chapter 3

The dominant role of individualism in the United States, especially compared with that in many European societies, can also be attributed to the country's status as a society of immigrants in another way. Unlike many European nations, citizenship in the United States, by definition, presupposes neither a family tradition within American society nor membership in a particular ethnic or religious community. What U.S. citizens share instead is a kind of enduring social contract based on the principles of freedom, the pursuit of happiness, and social mobility. This scaffolding was constructed around the dominant individualism as a means of creating a sense of common purpose and identity.

Initially, membership in U.S.-American society requires nothing more than the individual's political decision to become part of it. Membership in this national society is based on a free elective choice, not on shared historical background or inheritance—at least that is the idea. But an active form of freedom like this ideally presumes not only the absence of political and economic constraints but also the chance to select among a diverse array of possibilities. It is this individual voluntarism within American nationalism that also explains the central position of the market in particular. Culture and the market demonstrate their subservience to this value in the most trivial ways, by offering an endless and often meaningless multiplicity of consumer choices.

Self-determination and self-realization may be viewed as the main motor driving American individualism. They add up to a conviction grounded in the idea that inheritance and family background play much less of a role in an individual's success than that person's own decisions and ambitions. Again, this was at least the idea. Actual origins merely enrich a person's life; they do not decide his or her fate. In a society that envisions itself as constantly becoming, however, there is no redress for failure to achieve a better life. Failure, like success, is the individual's own doing. Social responsibility is played down. Sound familiar? Here, the basic values of American mythology are very much identical to the ideas behind economic liberalism.

The Glue that Binds Heterogeneous Societies

But individualism alone, even if everyone buys into this common denominator, can only carry a society so far. A minimum of social coordination is necessary where particular interests do not add up in a way that provides certain public goods such as a stable currency, a military, or functioning large-scale infrastructures. To emphasize unity and community, armies of politicians, historians, and experts on America have repeatedly attempted to discover a destiny or mission for the United States which, in turn, they retroactively interpreted as having been present at its genesis.

The roots of this political mythology are often traced back to John Winthrop, the governor of the Massachusetts Bay Colony, who, in a sermon he gave in 1630, came up with the phrase "shining city upon the hill" to describe the new colonies in North America, which he saw as the future of a new "God given" nation. These colonies, he said, were special: they even had a mission, namely, to live up to their special nature in the eyes of humanity.

Via the nineteenth-century political doctrine of manifest destiny, this idea grew into a sense of mission focused on Christianity, democracy, and human rights, in a specifically

American pattern that at certain moments has also served to justify an offensive and aggressive imperialism.[4] The core of this ideology has also been a blueprint for liberalism. According to Roger Cohen, it is centered on "its universalist embodiment of liberty, democracy, the rule of law and free enterprise."[5] Thus, the myth of the "shining city upon the hill" not only radiates out; it also seeks to integrate within, by helping create elements of commonality.

Others have proposed that a similar function of integration amid social diversity is to be found in an exceptional political culture of civic religion. The concept of civic religion goes back to Jean-Jacques Rousseau (1712–1778). It was picked up again in the 1960s by sociologist Robert N. Bellah as a way to describe specific functions of American society.[6] What Bellah meant by the term was a firmly established, institutionalized religion that does its work alongside the churches and is clearly distinguished from them—in short, a general religiosity in the political sphere that can provide social cohesion in an immigrant society.

Among the most prominent examples, we can surely cite presidential speeches, which invoke the constantly recurring theme of American destiny under God ("In God We Trust") in a way that is quasi-ritualistic. Together with other national symbols, such as the American flag or the national anthem, symbols with strong biblical connotations are also called upon to create a sense of common destiny. These civic religious symbols, Bellah noted, are observed mainly in public life and not within America's numerous religious communities. The religious spirit, invoked in everyday rituals, becomes a binding force.

In the past, the power of the unifying myths was greater. Belief in a shared history was especially pronounced in the postwar period—so pronounced, in fact, that anyone who was excluded from this unifying history was exposed to criticism. Since the rise of neoliberalism, however, these myths of social unity have become fragmented. Notions of the individual pursuit of happiness have dispelled all notions of community. That the crisis of democracy is especially pronounced in the United States is very decisively linked to the country's own self-concept, in which precisely this central tension is embedded.

From the vantage point of economic liberalism, society's base rests primarily on those people who, through their activities in the private market, generate the resources needed for living a good life. The government is basically charged with a single responsibility: providing the legal framework for the market's economic interactions and thus securing them. Other than this, government is supposed to do everything it can to stay out of the lives of its citizens and out of the market. Intervention in the distribution of income and wealth tends to be rejected. Accordingly, everything that the state is criticized for doing is referred to as "big government." This means first of all the federal government, that is, Washington, D.C., nowadays also known as "the swamp."

Thus, it is not surprising when the level of economic inequality that U.S. citizens find acceptable is far greater than it is, for example, in many European countries. If you believe in social mobility and in the corresponding dream that a dishwasher can become a millionaire, then you are also more inclined to accept unequal distribution within society. After all, you hope that one day you will be one of those on top! But citizens, ultimately, do not have limitless faith in their own chances for social advancement. If the economy and Wall Street are celebrating one party after another and the citizens are not invited, then the dream turns to rejection. Members of the meritocratic leadership are then perceived as a corrupt elite that refuses to give normal citizens access to the political process and to economic resources.

Community Crumbles

Tocqueville saw two main dangers in the special emphasis that is placed on individuality in the United States. One danger was that it could lead to the fragmentation of society. If every individual were to pursue only his or her own private interests, no commonwealth could exist, and democracy would inevitably fail. So far, so clear. The other danger, though, was that the mass of individuals would exercise a tyranny of the majority over minorities and outsiders. In this case, democracy would become a problem: if there were no checks on the *demos*, it would become the source of arbitrary rule.

Tocqueville had one and the same solution for both dangers—one that for him also explained the unusual success of democracy in America. The necessary institutions would have to be created to make individuals into citizens: a free press, a government that remained close to its citizens at the local level, and a kind of religious spirit that would value the common weal above special interests. Looking at these factors, it is perhaps also clear why the crisis has emerged with such political clarity in the United States. Against a background of gaping inequalities, a polarized media landscape, and a disconnected elite, precisely these fundamental conditions seem to have become ever more corrupted.

Certainly, the sense of social responsibility has not been entirely destroyed. Many U.S. citizens are still active today in clubs or associations, perform voluntary public service, and engage in philanthropy. Robert Putnam, referring to this social engagement, speaks of "social capital," that is, trust, mutuality, and communal life in the form of voluntary associations.[7] What he means by this is that social interactions and shared activities, which can emerge through participation in such organizations, establish specific social norms that have broad economic and social significance. But he, too, has to concede that those networks of relations no longer function the way the idea of a civic religion imagines. In the wake of individualization, they no longer seem to have the same impact. The title of Putnam's book *Bowling Alone* offered a conceptual handle on this danger, while also criticizing the loss of social capital in American society.[8] A group sport had turned into an individual discipline.

The national self-concept, in other words, has two contradictory myths at its core: myths that are centered on the pursuit of individual happiness and freedom, and others that invoke the unity of a heterogeneous population. Both are based on the idea of the historical uniqueness of the United States, for only there can a group of such different immigrants merge into a nation—*e pluribus unum*—and each individual pursue his or her own happiness. Precisely this tension between the unity myths, which have a political dimension, and the narrative of individualism, which is very much oriented to a person's economic interest, establishes the difficult balance between political and economic liberalism, which has fallen out of equilibrium today.

Institutionalized Culture: The Residual Welfare State

What Tocqueville still describes in very abstract terms as democracy's dangers quickly becomes concrete when we turn our attention from national mythology to social policy.[9] America's founding myths are clearly reflected in the institutional structure of its public welfare systems and are a decisive reason for the intellectual and institutional crisis of democracy that is taking place today. The hope of small government and individual freedom is written into the social construction of the state in a way that now seems to threaten democracy.

Individual self-determination, as described above, is one side of the coin, and the word *self-reliance* is engraved on the other. Liberalism in the United States has distinctly libertarian elements—much more so than in Europe. Here, the possibility of getting ahead also includes the right to fail. The person who loses his or her job must have had the wrong qualifications or did not work hard enough. Failure is individually, not socially, derived; consequently, a person can only help him- or herself, and this help occurs privately and on the free market. Government and society once again play only secondary roles. For were government to intervene, it would only constrain individuals' freedom of action and create a paternalistic dependency that would further hinder their development—or so the argument runs.

Hard work pays: this idea is at the core of both the liberal tradition and the notion of individual responsibility.

In the labor market, citizens are supposed to generate the resources necessary to lead a fulfilled life. This type of social welfare model is called "residual" in the research since it generally steps in to help with social risks only when the market fails. There are state-supported and private insurance programs that protect against the social risks of aging, illness, and unemployment, whereby private insurance companies are especially dominant in the sphere of health. State-supported health programs are available to only two groups: Medicare for the elderly and Medicaid for the poor. Social insurance programs in old age (Social Security) and health care (Medicare) can still be more or less plausibly justified based on the principles of individualism and self-reliance. After all, a person has paid into these plans, and therefore he or she also deserves to receive the benefits if it becomes necessary someday.

For all other social programs, which are funded primarily by tax revenues, the principle of neediness is paramount. The potential recipient must prove that he or she fully depends on these benefits and that they are deserved. This principle harmonizes beautifully with the traditional distinction between the "deserving" and the "undeserving" poor. It also reflects the principles of individualism and individual responsibility.[10] As a young and healthy man or woman, a person is naturally not deserving because he or she would have the individual ability to work. A single mother with three children, however, might possibly be a case where government assistance would seem justified.

The residual welfare state, then, is not a generous host to begin with. The market, as the producer of all welfare, is central. Under specific conditions, yes, support for social welfare may be forthcoming, but as a rule such cases are subject to intensive testing and those who would like to draw on their benefits are then naturally subject to social stigma. From the start, they fall under a general suspicion of wanting to lie around in the social hammock at the expense of their hardworking fellow citizens.

If, based on these political traditions, America's social welfare systems were already heavily market oriented, they became much more so after the end of the Cold War, when the country embarked on the Third Way. The neoliberal shift that followed caused a system that was already tilting toward the private sector to become completely one-sided. Triumphant market liberalism at the turn of the millennium wiped out any kind of sociopolitically oriented social policy and thus paved the way for the crisis of democracy.

Reform and Institutional Crisis

The origins of this particular crisis dimension can be traced to the 1990s. Criticism of the social welfare system was so strong at the time that President Clinton, as a Democrat, began his term in office with the sloganeering call to "end welfare as we know it." And so he did, with energetic support from the Republican Party. The core of this reform was to "repeal and replace"—the phrase has a familiar ring to anyone who is reading the newspapers—the family support program known as Aid for Families with Dependent Children (AFDC). According to AFDC, certain persons, especially mothers with children, had a right to social benefits. With the elimination of AFDC and its replacement by a new program, Temporary Assistance for Needy Families (TANF), this right was revoked and a time limit for receiving benefits from this program was imposed. The key word here is "temporary": that is, two years at a time and for a maximum of five years, after which the federal government is no longer obliged to pay any benefits. Individual states may prolong this period and continue the benefits by drawing on their own budgets, but no one has a rights claim to such support.

Parallel to this, another mantra of neoliberal critique was introduced into the social welfare realm: activation. The central idea here was that programs, above all, should reintegrate benefit recipients into the labor market. A trampoline instead of a hammock! A lot of money was also made available for this, for example, for child care, retraining, and even a new car to get to the job in a nearby city. Alongside these positive stimuli, there were of course negative ones. Failure to follow the recommendations of the case manager results in a cut in benefits. In the worst case, the consequences are abstruse. If, for example, a single mother is receiving benefits and then gives birth to another child, these benefits are also cut. The logic behind this? After all, who would be this irresponsible!

The fetish of wage labor is clearly identifiable in all these programs and reforms. But it is founded on the assumption that the market, specifically the labor market, is actually able to carry out these functions—in other words, that it is capable of providing everyone with a wage and sustenance. If, as we have seen, someone fails, it is a matter of personal responsibility. Overall, these ideas have led to a situation where the United States, in general and especially in times of economic crisis, can protect its citizens only in the most rudimentary way from the failures of the market. In situations where a person loses a job and in cases of illness as well, there is the real threat of a rapid loss of social position, indebtedness, and in many cases personal bankruptcy.

The United States certainly does have a system in place that helps people facing specific social risks. But compared with European welfare models, it differs in two specific respects that magnify the problem of a faltering labor market. First, there is the significantly greater proportion of private social insurance. This is especially true of retirement and illness, as reflected in total expenditures for these programs. In the United States in 2013, according to figures provided by the Organization for Economic Cooperation and Development (OECD), the percentage of gross domestic product (GDP) devoted to private social expenditures was 11.4 percent. By comparison, in Germany, only 3.3 percent was spent on private social expenditures, and in the OECD countries, the average was a mere 2.6 percent. Second, the United States relies much more heavily than many European governments on the tax system to generate social benefits. This happens in two ways. On one hand, private social expenditures receive massive tax subsidies—from the purchase of a house to the cost of private retirement or health insurance. On the other hand, social benefits are also disbursed directly through the tax system. The most prominent example of the latter is the Earned Income Tax Credit (EITC), in other words, a tax credit on income.

The assumption, which is widespread in Germany, that in the United States there is no such thing as social security is therefore not correct as such. These statements, and others like it, are primarily based on statistics that look at public expenditures for social welfare. And in this category, truly, the United States does not shine. In a ranking of thirty-five OECD countries, the United States occupies a disappointing twenty-fourth place, a rank that accords with the popular assumption. But when private social expenditures and tax subsidies are taken into account, the United States suddenly takes second place in the same ranking, surpassed only by France. The cost of social welfare in the United States is thus much higher than is normally assumed in Europe.

Does this make the United States a better welfare state? Not by a long shot, which is precisely where the actual problem lies. It is clear how ineffective the American system is when it comes to redistributing income and thus to reducing the concomitant inequalities. Since the 1990s, this problem has only become more acute. But there is something else that emerges from these numbers: in the United States, government is much less seen as the creator of social benefits than it is in many European countries. Tax subsidies for private coverage? I earned it! Benefits from the earned income tax credit? I work hard, so I am entitled to this.

All this fits very well into the idea of the liberal tradition, but in the process it also weakens the legitimacy of public social benefits. The government does nothing that is visible, so it is hard to address it as the source of social benefits. As a covert or hidden welfare state, it does help people, but those who are being supported do not actually see the government acting in this position.[11] The liberal tradition is strengthened, while government saws away at the branch it is sitting on.

This is important because numerous studies have shown that successful social programs create a base of supporters. America's Social Security program for the elderly is a case in point. People acknowledge that the program works and has noticeably reduced poverty among the elderly. But if the state is not seen as the source of this kind of benefits, then it does not receive from its citizens the support and the mandate that are required to stabilize or further enlarge these programs.

As long as the market was in a position to guarantee, more or less, the promise of economic growth, wealth, and social mobility, people were happy to forget the role that the government was actually playing. But if things are not going well in the market, then paradoxically the government is the first to be found guilty. Something that could serve to legitimize it, namely, the provision of social welfare support, is then not even forgotten: it is unseen. No wonder that in the context of the labor market crisis and rising inequalities in the United States, the government, including its personnel, comes in for criticism: out with the political establishment! The government should do even less to influence the markets!

As long as the American dream is doing its job and the hard-working individual can move up economically and socially, the liberal system finds supporters. But the restructuring of the social welfare state has drastically reduced social mobility. When the labor market also fails, as it did in the years after 2008, then the system begins to falter, and trust in the market is lost. The reason why the financial crisis has had such long-term consequences is that it caused the problems of a residual welfare state and chronic inequality to escalate. The lack of future prospects, private indebtedness, and disappearing chances for social advancement sow seeds of dissatisfaction, while also creating fertile soil for populist mobilization.

All this is at the source of Washington's legitimation crisis. The government is supposed to be managed exactly like a corporation, and so an entrepreneur also seems like the best choice for the White House. Here, too, economic logic dominates. In the framework of the crisis of neoliberalism, it is the ideology of the liberal tradition that makes the United States so vulnerable right now. The lack of alternatives to liberalism is so firmly entrenched in people's heads that many would be happiest if the government could be completely privatized in order to return to a glorified era of Great Promises that actually never existed in that form. Make America great again!

The Economic Dimension of the Crisis

With the financial crisis, as stubborn inequalities grew even more acute and indeed nearly insuperable, the intellectual and institutional crisis of America's individualized market economy became a tangible problem. This problem currently seems to be developing into a long-term crisis of democracy. If we look at the distribution of income and wealth in the United States over the last forty years, the surprise and the frustration of the people who receive an increasingly small piece of the pie are understandable. Wages and incomes in the United States are currently as unevenly distributed as they were in the era of the Great Depression. Things are looking great for the top earners, who have done better and better in comparison to the rest of society. French economist Thomas Piketty and his colleagues have made clear that it is the top one percent, in particular, who have benefited most from economic development since the 1970s.[12] Bill Clinton's and George W. Bush's deregulation policies, starting in the 1990s, did stimulate free market forces for a certain period, but it was the rich, above all, who profited. The middle class and lower-income groups saw almost no rise in income.

The bottom 20 percent of income earners in the United States have been more or less shut out of the market for the last forty years when it comes to increases in income. Their average annual income in 2014, at $21,423, was a mere 2.7 percent greater than their income in 1974.[13] Over the same period, the income of the highest 10 percent jumped by a staggering 231 percent. The government, via its tax and transfer systems, did very little during this period to balance out this unequal distribution of market forces. On the contrary, tax reductions, for example, under George W. Bush in the years after 2000—or under Donald Trump in 2017, for that matter—made the spread between rich and poor even more extreme.

It is true that the average household income—income after taxes and social transfers—grew by about 62 percent during the period between 1979 and 2008, in other words, right up until the start of the financial and economic crisis. But here, too, as with market gains more generally, it took very different forms. The top earners (the top 1 percent) recorded an increase of 275 percent, and the top 20 percent saw a 64 percent increase. The middle class had to settle for an increase of 40 percent, while the bottom 20 percent received only 18 percent. As a result, the overall distribution of household income in 2007 was substantially more unequal than it had been at the end of the 1970s. Today, the incomes of the richest 20 percent account for a greater share of total income than those of the remaining 80 percent.

Middle-class and lower-income groups are the losers in this development. Their share of total income has decreased continuously in recent decades. A look at the top earners illustrates this development in exemplary fashion. In the 1970s, the share of total income going to the top 1 percent was still around 10 percent, and the bottom half of the population was still able to reach 20 percent of total income. Today, the picture is completely inverted: 20 percent of all income goes to the top 1 percent, and 13 percent to the bottom 50 percent. A glance at salaries is also instructive. In the 1960s, a manager, on average, took home approximately 24 times what the average employee and worker in his or her firm earned. In 2009, in the midst of the crisis, a CEO took home 185 times as much income at the end of the year as the company's employees.

To a large extent, this development can be laid at the feet of American tax policy, which has clearly become more regressive in the most recent decades. The difference in the effective tax rates of rich and poor has become noticeably less, since corporate and property taxes were greatly reduced (mainly in the 1990s) and individual contributions to social security went up. Under Obama, this trend was temporarily halted. He allowed the massive tax reductions of the Bush administration, which mainly benefited the top earners, to expire, and he introduced an additional tax on the rich to help finance his health care reform. For many U.S. citizens, however, this did not go far enough. They voted for Donald Trump because he promised to give the government of the United States back to the citizens.

Chapter 3

Precisely this toxic mixture of deregulation, tax reductions for the rich, and cuts in welfare programs created the basis for dissatisfaction and a loss of trust among broad sectors of society. Combined with the national ideological overemphasis on individualism and self-reliance, ideas and ideologies were able to take root in the public discourse that ultimately led to social division and, quite concretely, to the 2008 financial and economic crisis. This crisis was as serious as it was because it brought an already porous social system, which is dependent on growth, to the edge of collapse. If we wanted to tie it to a specific development, we could say that today's crisis of democracy is an aftershock of this same financial crisis.

The Global Financial Crisis of 2008

In the midst of the electoral contest between Barack Obama and John McCain in 2007, the news broke of the bankruptcy of Lehman Brothers. Stock markets all over the world crashed, immense fortunes were destroyed, and the real estate market in the United States completely collapsed. Obama saw the need to act and offered his help to then President George W. Bush. A crisis of this magnitude, he thought, demanded bipartisan cooperation. The voters seemed to recognize this. For the first time, Obama passed McCain in the polls, and he also succeeded in bringing this advantage safely through the homestretch. Obama's move into the White House, however, was accompanied by one of the biggest financial and economic crises in nearly a hundred years.

Much has been written about the crisis in the meanwhile; the U.S. Congress even established a commission to investigate its causes. The Financial Crisis Inquiry Commission concluded in its final report that this crisis could have been avoided. The report named human actions and failure to act. It criticized the administration and its financial oversight practices, while focusing equally on Wall Street's reckless risk management. Actually, politicians should have seen the warning signals sooner: unethical practices in banks' awarding of credit, the dramatically increased indebtedness of private households, and an inadequately regulated trade in financial derivatives.

Ultimately, the crisis occurred due to the expansive monetary policy of the Federal Reserve and high capital flows. After the bursting of the dot-com bubble in the year 2000 and the terror attacks of 2001, the U.S. Federal Reserve continued to pump massive amounts of money into the economy, despite the fact that it was already recovering. There seemed to be no other solution to the fact that the labor market did not recover to the same extent and there was persistent high unemployment. In addition, the Fed continued for too long to underestimate the price bubble in the American real estate market.

Low interest rates, together with the possibility of passing on mortgage risk through securitization and asset-backed securities, encouraged the real estate bubble to become even bigger and, at the same time, led to a loosening of credit and mortgage standards for borrowers who in point of fact could not afford them (subprime loans). Low interest rates fueled an increase in debt-financed consumption, and as a result purchases of real estate became even more attractive. A large part of the precrisis economic success in the United States is attributable to strong domestic consumption, which, however, was paid for with enormous private indebtedness. This sort of model is only stable if real estate prices continue to climb, while at the same time interest rates remain low. When real estate prices declined, the whole system collapsed.

The failure of the financial markets—a result of their excessive appetite for risk—was initially made possible by the ineffectiveness of government regulation, since the 1990s. The financial sector responded to deregulation by developing more and more new financial products as a means of remaining competitive in the increasingly international financial markets. Along with the above-mentioned asset-backed securities, we have to mention credit default swaps, which were supposed to make credit risks safer. On one hand, this financial product did make high yields possible; on the other, however, it led to a decoupling of creditors and borrowers. As a result, possible risks were ignored, covered up, or rendered simply no longer recognizable within the complex structures of financial transactions. Faith in new processes of mathematical computation; the actions of rating agencies, which gave top billing to all the new financial products; and conscious financial fraud then ultimately created the distortions in the financial markets that led first to a banking crisis and finally to a crisis in the real economy.

But all that is only one side of the story. The other is a failure of financial oversight and thus of U.S. policy, both of which believed for too long in the self-regulating and self-healing powers of the market. Exactly as in the case of the country's social welfare and education policies, a fanatical belief in the market led to a highly problematic retreat of the government. The new financial products were seen first of all as evidence of the innovative power of financial markets, while deregulation, since the 1990s, was thought to be contributing to the growing strength of America's finance sector. Oversight of finance has traditionally been weak in the United States: the market itself has simply been considered more important. Hence, before the crisis, there was no regulatory authority that bore overall responsibility. A variety of oversight bodies did keep watch over the banking sector, the stock market, and insurance. But this bewildering field of regulators and regulated created strong conflicts of interest as many actors frequently switched sides, either from oversight to the private market or vice versa. These revolving doors were a significant factor in the calamitous lack of regulation and turned a risky situation into a dangerous one.

The crisis in real estate also had such immense consequences because in the United States home ownership plays a much bigger role than it does in Germany, for example. Here, again, we see an inflection of the "American dream," the idea of self-reliance, which is best expressed in private ownership—the so-called ownership society. The crisis struck a social system where, as we have seen, the political framework already evinced a tendency toward private care and individual responsibility, a system that, with the triumph of economic liberalism in recent decades, had turned every possibility to soften the crisis into the responsibility of individuals.

Obama did attempt to push back. When it comes to expenditures for welfare and other social benefits, the years 2009 and 2010 (after the financial crisis) are clear outliers if we compare them, for example, with the cuts in welfare benefits and the market-friendly restructuring of labor that had taken place in the 1990s and 2000s. In the framework of the programs Obama created in response to the recession, the federal government actually increased funding for social welfare by almost a fifth. An additional emergency fund for TANF, totaling $7 billion, was also intended to give individual states the means to provide needier individuals not only with monetary support but also with subsidized jobs. The requirements and restrictions that had been imposed in the course of the 1996 welfare reform were not loosened, however.

Federal funds for food stamps were increased by $19.9 billion, meaning that monthly benefits went up by approximately $80 per recipient. Although the antirecessionary program did help a significant number of U.S. citizens cope with the negative effects of the economic crisis—not least because it extended the length of eligibility for unemployment benefits—it did not represent a longer-term solution to the numerous problems surrounding poverty and the evident shortcomings of the social safety net. Moreover, the explosion of costs after the crisis produced a perfidious reaction: Obama was accused of having incurred too many debts, so that the federal budget would need to be cut back to make the country competitive again—an argument that Trump was only too happy to pick up once his moment had come.

Dependent on the Market

The economic and financial crisis made very clear the extent to which American's socioeconomic model is dependent on a dynamic labor market and, more specifically, on a constantly growing low-wage sector. If the latter is no longer able to absorb as many people, as happened during the current economic crisis, the country's already quite fragile social balance comes under threat. The 2016 presidential campaign also demonstrated this very clearly. In the camps of both political parties, candidates mobilized based on the difficult economic situation. Sanders led a primary campaign among Democrats that was mainly focused on the growing social and economic inequalities, and Donald Trump was able to attract voters and win votes especially in those regions where the economic recovery was least felt and the unemployment rate had climbed far above the national average.

Fundamental distrust in government has turned into an attitude of refusal that makes the administration responsible for everything that goes wrong but that simultaneously fails to acknowledge that it was precisely the cutbacks in public social support systems that lit the fire under the crisis and then blew on it. In the economic liberals' thought model, it is not just that government plays a subordinate role. When it comes to politics and public affairs, there is virtual amnesia about the role that the American government has played up until now. This, at least, is the conclusion drawn by American political scientists Jacob Hacker and Paul Pierson in their 2016 book *American Amnesia*.[14] This memory loss is not somehow accidental. It derives, as we have seen, from the political culture of the United States and has been used strategically by powerful special interests to advance their agendas. This includes mega-actors in private enterprise, above all Wall Street finance capital, which has been able to impose its interests by means of massive lobbying. The Republican Party, too, employs this line of argument as a means of generating political support.

For a long time in America's history, its citizens cultivated a healthy skepticism toward government in general but on the whole found ways to live with its evils. Those times seem to be over. People on the conservative political spectrum, in particular, no longer seem to want to come to any kind of accommodation with the scourge that is the state. At the same time, more progressive authors, such as Hacker and Pierson, are by no means committed to a socialist utopia when it comes to the state. They sketch out a nuanced picture of a mixed economy in which the government intervenes effectively to regulate market mechanisms, provides the necessary infrastructure, and invests in research and development, from which the private market ultimately benefits.

As late as the 1950s, this was acknowledged by many U.S. citizens. That there could be no free markets without state intervention was a matter for consensus. In his first State of the Union address, President Dwight D. Eisenhower mentioned the administration almost forty times (!) and almost always with a positive connotation. The big companies also saw the government more as a partner than as an opponent. Under the aegis of the Committee for Economic Development, such corporations as Kodak and General Motors worked closely with the government to find solutions to the most pressing economic problems. This was the core of the Fordist compromise, which Ronald Reagan cancelled, at the latest, in the 1980s. For him, the worst words in the English language were "I'm from the government and I'm here to help."

When the Republicans proved successful at mobilizing around this antigovernment rhetoric, the Democrats also fell in line. Bill Clinton, in his first State of the

Union address, mentioned the administration only half as often as Eisenhower, and mostly with negative connotations. Clinton actually went so far as to declare that the era of "big government" had come to an end. According to Hacker and Pierson, the United States is now paying the price for this rightward move by both parties. In international rankings of social progress, for example, in the areas of health and education, the United States is trending downward. In early childhood education, America ranks only twenty-fifth among OECD countries. Studies of social mobility and living standards also confirm the suspicion that the liberal dreams of the millennium have not come to fruition in the United States. But many people lack awareness of the causes of this crisis and seek responsibility in themselves or in the overloaded administration rather than in structural problems—problems that, at the moment, are only becoming more firmly entrenched.

The Future of Work

After the unprecedented shock that the financial crisis administered to an already-fragile social system, it is the crisis of work that probably represents the biggest economic threat to democracy in the United States. Because welfare benefits were tied to gainful employment, the financial and economic crisis set off a massive downward spiral that made the status quo feel no longer bearable for many people. For this reason, the ten years since the crisis can be described as a lost decade for the labor market. Since then, the earned income of most American families is stagnating, while the impact of economic growth has been felt above all in the bank accounts of the superrich.

Chapter 3

Back in 2001, the United States had already been hit by a recession. It was much less serious than the one that would follow seven years later, but it took until 2017 for wages to begin to recover, albeit very slowly and in a highly unequal manner.[15] When the next economic crisis struck in 2007, wages were still noticeably lower than before the economic crisis of 2001, despite the fact that the years between 2001 and 2007 saw notable rates of economic growth.

Not only did economic developments and public policy lead to a growing gap between wages and salaries, but the labor market was no longer functioning as a motor of social advancement. In international comparisons, the image of the United States as the land of unlimited opportunities, where a person with initiative and talent can break through all class barriers, has suffered grievous damage. When it comes to social mobility, the United States today ranks only thirteenth on a list of seventeen other OECD countries. Only Slovenia, Chile, Italy, and Great Britain have performed worse. With this, the United States, badly outmatched, lags behind such countries as Denmark, Finland, Norway, or even Canada. In general, U.S. citizens today end up in the same economic class as the one they started out in, and the same will also be true of future generations. In numbers, two of three children in families with low incomes will see no social advancement.

To this is added the structural disadvantage of specific groups, who in 2016 were unable to persuade themselves to vote for Hillary Clinton and "more of the same," and stayed home. Thus, the unemployment rates of Hispanics and African Americans between 1979 and 2011 were notably higher than those of white Americans. The structural disadvantage experienced by African Americans is also evident from other figures. The year 1992 is considered the one in which the wealth of African Americans came closest to that of whites, although even then the wealth of African American households amounted to all of 16.8 percent of that of white households. When the mortgage bubble burst, that value fell to a barely imaginable 5 percent.

Along with these ethnic minorities, there were also many women who did not vote for Hillary Clinton. They, too, had not benefited sufficiently from the Third Way and the politics of no alternatives to muster any enthusiasm for the status quo—even when, for the first time in American history, there was the chance to elect a female president. And even if the pay gap between men and women had decreased in recent decades, this was only partly because the situation was improving for women. Instead, men were losing ground, which ultimately led to a more equal distribution of wages between men and women: the logic of neoliberal justice!

In the meanwhile, the unemployment rate has fallen back down to where it was before the crisis, although it is true that many people have had to settle for jobs that pay less, and the recovery looks very different in different regions of the United States. It is not only wages and salaries that paint a clear picture of the crisis in the labor market. Between 2000 and 2007, the unemployment rate averaged about 4 percent. In 2010, when the effects of the crisis were being felt most strongly, it had risen to 9.6 percent; by 2011 it had fallen only to 8.9 percent. Observers have generally noted the very slow recovery in the labor market. And even in those sectors that did experience some improvements in the last couple of years, the recovery was mainly due to a massive expansion of the low-wage labor market and a very high long-term unemployment ratio.

We can also talk about a crisis of work more generally, for less and less work is needed. This could also make the crisis of democracy into a persistent problem. Until now, long-term unemployment has largely been an unknown phenomenon in the United States, chiefly because of America's unregulated labor market, which functions according to the principle "hire and fire." If it is possible to fire employees soon after they are hired, this also means that there are incentives to hire them: this is the customary justification for the flexibilization of labor. In the United States, a person is considered to be long-term unemployed if he or she has been looking for work for more than twenty-seven weeks. In the early 1990s, only every tenth unemployed person was categorized as long-term unemployed. By 2007, however, every fifth unemployed person had been looking for a job for more than twenty-seven weeks, and in 2010 it was almost every second one. Currently, the long-term unemployed ratio is around 25 percent—significantly higher than before the economic crisis. Under such conditions, labor markets do not work flexibly.

In reality, the problem is even bigger. The unemployment figures include only those individuals who are actively seeking work. The labor force participation rate, in contrast, includes everyone between twenty-five and fifty-four years of age, the period when people are generally available to the labor market. Shortly before the economic crisis, the labor force participation rate was 66.4 percent, according to the Bureau of Labor Statistics. By 2010, it had fallen to 64.8 percent and dropped further down to 62.7 percent in 2018.

For Trump voters, the guilty parties who were responsible for this debacle were easy to identify: globalization and the shifting of jobs to countries where businesses could manufacture things more cheaply. During the election, Trump promised to bring these jobs back to the United States. This allowed him to mobilize especially effectively in those regions that had been hardest hit by the shifting of jobs overseas. Whether he can keep this promise is something Trump will still have to demonstrate. Many experts start from the assumption that even if companies were to bring jobs back to the United States, the extent to which this would create new jobs would be very limited, since in many industries robots now do the work better and more cheaply than people. Technological modernization is one of the main reasons why there are fewer and fewer jobs in industrial production, especially low-paid jobs. This predicament will persist after Trump.

The Political Crisis

The cultural crisis of deep individualization and social fragmentation by itself could have been overcome. From a U.S.-American perspective, after all, it is the normal state of affairs. It was the economic crisis that had first turned inequality into a problem for the meritocratic style of American liberalism. But it is the political crisis of the United States that is actually at the core of the crisis of democracy. Economic inequalities have become political inequalities. Against the background of polarization, the structure of the political system itself has become a source of instability.. The built-in blocking mechanisms, which are actually supposed to guarantee democracy, have led to a democratic standstill instead. The model democracy turned its own weapons against itself, with corrosive consequences.

A number of very different developments have created a tangled skein of problems that fundamentally calls into question the qualification of the United States as a democracy. Thus, political scientists Martin Gilens and Benjamin Page also ask whether the category "oligarchy" would not be more apt for the United States at this time. Gilens and Page's concerns center on the opportunities citizens have to influence politics, for example, the extent to which elected officials, in their actions and policies, act in accordance with the interests of the people who elected them. Political scientists call this "responsiveness."[16] In the United States, elected representatives are no longer attuned to the interests of the middle class or of low-income groups. They now listen only to the interests of the superrich and the organized special interests that, with their campaign contributions and lobbying, succeed in influencing politics "inside the beltway" of Washington, D.C. Economic inequality thus also translates into unequal access to political participation, and this is a problem even for the most liberal U.S. citizens. If the government only listens to the very wealthy, then policies are implemented that also correspond to their interests. Politics becomes circular; economic inequality increases.

Under these circumstances, democracy's correction mechanism—elections—is ineffective. The only way to break open this circle seems to be either to carry out a political revolution (Sanders) or to drain the swamp (Trump). This perspective also makes abundantly clear that the neoliberal politics of the last thirty years in America—the curtailment of the welfare state, the deregulation of markets, and massive tax reductions for the very well-off—was not a politics to which there were no alternatives but a concession to the superrich and the powerful interest groups that succeeded in getting the ear of the political system. All this has come at the expense of the middle class and low-income groups, whom no one listened to anymore, and who now want to make themselves heard again by voting for radical political forces.

The influence of money in politics plays a decisive role in the lack of responsiveness. Elections in the United States are expensive, and the politicians have to get this money from somewhere (not all of them are as rich as Donald Trump). The average cost of running for a seat in the House of Representatives, today, is $1 million. Everyone who wants to protect his or her position has to collect this amount of money again every two years. Ten times this amount—that is, $10 million—is what a campaign for a seat in the Senate costs. In the presidential election between Obama and Mitt Romney in 2012, the two campaigns each spent more than $1 billion. It makes a person wonder where this money comes from. The answer is perhaps unsurprising, but crucial nonetheless.

In 2012, more than 40 percent of all private contributions to the election came from the richest 0.01 percent in terms of income. In the 1980s, this percentage from the superrich was only 10 percent! Generally speaking, both parties profited from the contributions, although the Republicans had a slight advantage: 62 percent of these campaign contributions ended up in their election accounts. The system of electoral finance is generally strictly regulated and formally transparent—at least where the specific electoral team is concerned. In this case, there are firm rules about how much money you can give to candidates, parties, and other groups during an election. But alongside this, since 2008, another realm of election financing has grown, which is concerned not with the expenditures of the various candidates and their campaigns but with third parties that are not permitted to be directly linked to the campaigns. This area is known as "independent expenditures," and here we again encounter influential and financially powerful actors and special-interest groups that seek to influence elections. In 2010, the Supreme Court gave these actors the constitutional right, under the hallowed concept of freedom of expression, to spend as much money as they want to. And since then this is what they do.

If these independent expenses in 2008 totaled $200 million, by 2012 they had risen to $1 billion—a fivefold increase in only two years. Thank you, *Citizens United*! The name of this Supreme Court decision has since become part of the vocabulary of political discussion. Most of these expenditures are made by so-called super PACs (political action committees), which are groups founded especially to promote specific elections or interests as a means of influencing the election. Naturally, the super PACs also get their money from the superrich. In the year 2012, 93 percent of these financial contributions came from only 3,381 individuals—around 60 percent from just 159 individuals. This is a relatively easy-to-identify group of people on whom the politicians have to focus if they want to find the financial resources needed to conduct a successful campaign. The elections themselves then become a sideshow, and the interests of the voters come in second.

Polarization

But the influence of money is not the only problem bedeviling the American political system, even if it is certainly one of the gravest when it comes to the quality of democracy. The buzzwords *polarization* and *gridlock* are often used to describe other aspects of the political crisis that have resulted from the inequalities. Compromises no longer seem possible, and a politics of ideological extremism is taking over. This phenomenon is not entirely new, but it has become institutionally fixed and threatens to explode the political discourse altogether.[17]

As early as the 1990s, the phenomenon of polarization was being talked about as a *culture war*—the buzzword for a cultural battle being waged by the two political camps. At the center of this "war" were abortion, the right to bear arms, the separation of church and state, drugs, and homosexuality. Around these questions, two poles formed within the political discourse. These two poles can no longer discuss things with each other on a common basis. Since the 1990s, the split in society has even expanded beyond the above-named issues: ideology became *Weltanschauung*. At the core of the division, once again, we often find the familiar question about what role the central government should play in the United States.

This division of society into two camps becomes problematic because in the meanwhile the media landscape has adapted to it.[18] Under the pressure to sell their news programs, in other words, to attract stable consumer groups that will generate advertising revenue, the media come up with exactly those messages their consumers want to hear. Right-leaning media such as Fox News complain about the government and Democratic politicians, in particular. Obama, for the right-wing media, was the incarnation of evil. Now, left-leaning media, for example, MSNBC, see Trump the same way. After his 2012 electoral victory, Obama said that if he had watched Fox News all day, he would not have voted for his reelection. If you watch the news on the two stations, in fact you will not get the impression that you are hearing about the same country.

Stations that once used to be politically neutral, like CNN, are ground down by this competitive struggle. They carry on 24-7 with "breaking news," as a means of maintaining their market share among media consumers. Scandal-mongering and one-sided reportage are the result. Now the only media outlet that is trusted is the one that broadcasts the messages a person wants to hear; people scarcely venture out of these echo chambers. Everything the other side reports is disqualified as "fake news." In Germany, right-wing populists refer to comparable but still noticeably tamer developments as "*Lügenpresse*," or "lying press"—a term that has unmistakable Nazi overtones. What gets left in the dust in the battle of opinions is quality journalism, whose well-researched and balanced reporting gives citizens the information they need to make political decisions. For this, neither the time nor the market is available now. The public is divided in half, and the two parts no longer communicate; they only shout at each other.

Naturally, this is not inconsequential for the work of Congress. It is a big problem especially for a presidential system, in which parties actually are not intended to play such a strong role. The political system in the United States is candidate focused. This means first of all that people, not parties, get elected. Party lists of the kind that exist in Germany are unknown in the United States. Candidates organize their own run for office, raise their own funds, and are ultimately responsible to their constituencies. Parties usually only get involved in supportive ways, by offering a broader, philosophical worldview within which voters can place their candidates. This system, naturally, also makes the elected official more independent from the party organization or legislative fraction. This is the tradition.

No wonder then that in the 1960s a Republican congressman only voted with his party about 60 percent of the time. Among the Democrats, this occurred only half the time. The electoral district at home was much more important, in keeping with the politician's interest in being reelected two or six years hence. In this sense, members of Congress in the United States have been like "church steeple" politicians, who are only concerned about their home district and thus look no farther than they can see from the church steeple of their own congregation. Questions of *Weltanschauung* and the big questions of politics played a secondary role in their voting behavior. Of course, this picture is simplified and exaggerated, but it explains a phenomenon that has been central to the way politics works in the United States, namely, the motivation and the will to forge compromises and coalitions that are not party-bound and that vary according to the given topic and problem. And this has worked, as the above-cited figures show. But the situation has undergone a massive change.

Today, coalitions or compromises with political opponents are as good as impossible, especially when it comes to the kinds of issues that also divide society. In the House of Representatives today, 90 percent of Democrats and Republicans vote with their party bloc. Some commentators see the polarization of the political elites as a direct consequence of the polarization of society. Others, though, believe reforms within Congress that led to the exercise of stronger control by party leaders are partly responsible for it. In this way, they argue, an informal but effective discipline has developed within the party factions, which makes nonpartisan compromises hugely more difficult. Yet others explain the polarization of the political elites by the structure of electoral districts. In recent years, thanks to gerrymandering and sorting, electoral districts have become more and more homogenous and hence less politically contested. As a result, moderate candidates are no longer as successful. Radicalism pays because the actual electoral decisions are no longer made in the election itself but instead in the primaries, since it is quite certain that one party—or the other—will win the district. This could explain developments in the House of Representatives, at least. In the Senate, it is true, the electoral districts are whole states; and yet there, too, we see clear signs of polarization.

Probably the best explanation is one that takes all these factors into account. What is important, though, is that these developments have very definitely led to a political standstill and a gridlock of the political system. The established mechanisms within the political system no longer correspond to the polarization of the parties. Media polarization both mirrors this problem and renders it more acute, making it more and more difficult to put together a successful politics. The blockade no longer serves as an instrument of the weaker side, as it was conceived. It is turning from an instrument for ensuring the democratic decentralization of power into a permanent state of exception. Politics is becoming inefficient and untrustworthy; the actual intent of the political apparatus has been transformed into its opposite.

The System Cancels Itself Out

The so-called founding fathers, the men who participated actively in writing the Constitution, established a political system that was designed, on one hand, to minimize the influence of the citizens on politics but, on the other hand, to prevent the concentration of political power. This goal, which at first glance appears self-contradictory, can be explained based on the historical context of the United States in the late eighteenth century. It is also the reason why the political system is stumbling today.

On one side, the writers of the Constitution wanted to distance themselves from Great Britain as their former colonial power. They felt the newly created nation should be more democratic, and the emerging institution of the presidency should be clearly differentiated from the British monarchy. But naturally the writers of the Constitution themselves belonged to the political and social elite of that era, and they feared the power of the mob. For this reason, the political offices in the newly created government were to be democratically legitimated, but not directly elected, by the people.

The Electoral College is an institutionalized form of this idea. But it has become a problem, because under the present circumstances it undermines the legitimacy of the government. For a long time, the results of the Electoral College always coincided with the popular vote. In the course of the increasing polarization of American society, which was leading to closer and closer results in presidential elections, some people actually even praised the Electoral College because it turned close electoral victories into clear wins. Thus, in 2008, for example, Obama was barely able to defeat John McCain in the popular vote, with a showing of 52.9 percent. But in the Electoral College, he won a majority of 67.8 percent. Such majorities give the incoming president greater legitimation and thus a means of carrying out a political agenda.

But now, given the extreme polarization, all this has changed, and the legitimacy of the political process has suffered as a result. In the last five presidential elections, there were two times when the result of the popular vote did *not* coincide with the vote of the Electoral College. In the 2000 election, Al Gore, a Democrat, got 543,895 more votes than his Republican competitor, George W. Bush. In the Electoral College, however, Bush won the vote, 271 to 266. The final decision fell to Florida. There, because of the closeness of the results, the votes had to be recounted in individual electoral districts. Ultimately, the legal battle landed in the Supreme Court, which halted the recounts on December 12, 2000, and awarded the state's Electoral College votes to Bush, thus securing his victory.

The second case is present to everyone's mind. Donald Trump won a clear victory, with 304 Electoral College votes; his competitor, Hillary Clinton, received only 227. However, in the popular vote, Clinton had an advantage of almost three million votes (2.1 percent) over Trump. For this reason, many Democrats do not accept that Trump's election was legitimate. The fact that the chances of changing the electoral procedure are slim, thanks to the intentionally high hurdles placed in the path of changes to the Constitution, does not exactly enhance respect for the country's democratic institutions.

The separation of powers is a second sensitive point where the crisis is manifested. The architects of the U.S. Constitution built in numerous (temporal, horizontal, and vertical) control mechanisms in addition to the Electoral College in order to prevent the abuse of power or the concentration of power in a single political institution. If, today, the process of electing a president casts doubt on the legitimacy of the result, the structure of the state apparatus is limiting the president's effectiveness.

This provision, too, was actually intended to strengthen democracy, but today it delegitimizes government's actions. The result of the separation of powers is a multiplicity of interests that are in conflict with one another. At the same time, the political parties lack the instruments that could structure heterogeneous institutions and actors. This is all the more problematic because the American system of reciprocal control strictly separates the powers of the three branches of government, although in the exercise of political power they need to cooperate with each other. The institutions act independently but are simultaneously compelled to cooperate. This becomes particularly clear in the process of passing legislation. Here, the functions of the two legislative chambers intersect and overlap the same way those of the executive and legislative branches do. The legislative branch is the central political institution of the United States: the Constitution describes its powers before those of the president. Congress, consisting of the Senate and the House of Representatives, is invested with the power to make laws.

In a parliamentary system such as Germany's, the government is dependent on the support of the majority of members of Parliament, meaning that Parliament is able to exert a high degree of control over the administration. In the American presidential system, the intersecting power structure lacks this component. The president is independent of the legislative majority. Still, the legislative branch has various possibilities for exerting control over the executive, that is, the president. If the president commits "high crimes and misdemeanors," he can be impeached. Signatures of presidents on international treaties are only valid if they have also been ratified by the Senate. Moreover, the Senate must approve the appointment of top officials (judges, ambassadors, secretaries of federal departments). Among Congress's most effective control mechanisms is the "power of the purse": Congress must approve the federal budgets and can cut them. A president without financial resources is a powerless president.

All this generally contributes to the success of democracy, since power is in fact decentralized. Today, many people may be singing a hymn in praise of the separation of powers, for it is this that makes many of Trump's projects fail or at least holds them back—from the Muslim ban to the repeal of the Affordable Care Act (Obamacare). The blockade was also something that was considered desirable back when the republic was founded, but it was not supposed to bring things to a standstill. The system was devised at a time when there were not yet any political parties, and no polarization as we know it today. But given the extreme polarization of American politics, this is precisely what has happened: the established structures of the political system have become a straitjacket and turned the separation of powers and other pillars of democracy into a problem—so much so that the functioning of democracy has become partially impossible and its democratic institutions themselves have become a danger for democracy.

Against the background of a blocked Congress, where the Republicans did not hesitate to push their own economy to the brink of the infamous fiscal cliff, the political class seems to have delegitimated itself. Why get involved politically if market thinking's line of approach offers no alternatives anyway, and when almost every political initiative runs aground in the institutional labyrinth of the nation's capital? Congress seemed to be rejecting its own competence, and the political process went nowhere in all too many cases, while inequalities continued to grow and possibilities for advancement disappeared. The longing for outsiders against this backdrop is not very surprising. Perhaps, after all, someone could really clean house in Washington?

Losers and Winners

If, for a long time, right-wing populism was more of a marginal social phenomenon, with Donald Trump it has definitively arrived in the political center. During his campaign, Trump employed populist rhetorical elements and used them successfully to mobilize a broad spectrum of forces and movements. The Republican Party has a long history of using the narrative of "us against them at the top" in combination with appeals to nativist or racist attitudes. Nixon and his "Southern Strategy" sought the support of white voters in the South with racist rhetoric. Ronald Reagan demonized black welfare recipients to galvanize the electorate in the white suburbs. Until now, however, this political opportunism was not sufficient to characterize the Republican Party in its entirety. It was only with the Tea Party and its fundamental critique of Obama's presidency that the ideological ground was prepared for Trump's electoral campaign. With this, Trump moved right-wing populism from the margins of society to the political center.

He used it to mobilize successfully among the traditional radical right in the United States but also within the white working and middle classes, which in the past had tended to vote Democratic. This was the very group that saw its social status being threatened by the increasing international integration of markets. They saw a way out in the new economic nationalism and in closing the country off to immigrants, as Trump promised. In the regions with high unemployment, in industrial suburbs of the so-called Rust Belt, he promised that he would bring back their old jobs (while never, in his promises, saying a word about social standards and benefits of these jobs). At the same time, he whipped up fears of inner-city unrest (a reference to the racial conflicts of the 1970s) and external threats (ISIS and the southern border) to mobilize his supporters. To the surprise of some, Trump never abandoned this mode of political campaigning and has kept on agitating since he entered office.

The crisis of democracy in the United States is as visible as it is because economic liberalism was already so pronounced there. The culture of individualism, the drastically increased inequalities that followed the financial crisis, and the growing polarization have driven the existing political structures to the brink of dysfunctionality.

Polarization within the political system had become even more drastic during Obama's presidency. Shortly after his election, the Republicans had already announced a total blockade against any and all of his legislative initiatives. In his first two years, Obama could still govern with a Democratic majority in both houses of Congress, which also makes him one of the most successful legislative presidents in U.S. history. We tend to forget that his legislative success rate, in those years, was actually around 90 percent. But after the midterm elections in 2010, when the Republicans secured a majority in the House of Representatives, Obama's rate of success fell to around 20 percent.

The polarization of the political parties in the United States has had a dual effect on political effectiveness. If one party controls both the executive branch and both houses of Congress (unified government), then it is possible to govern effectively. If one of the houses of Congress is controlled by a different party than the one the president belongs to, this leads to a blockade of the political system. Until recently, this would have been the accepted crisis narrative for U.S. politics. But, with Trump, it has finally become clear that the crisis affecting the political parties runs much deeper than was previously assumed. Both parties are internally disunited and are wearing themselves out in internal fights with their own extremes.

By now, both parties are mutually blocked. Despite a Republican majority in both houses of Congress until the 2018 midterms, Trump was barely able to keep even one of his central legislative promises in the first two years of his presidency. Trumpcare, the attempt to repeal Obamacare, was too extremist for the Republicans Party's moderate wing but did not go far enough for the Tea Party faction. As a result, in this case and in others, the political majorities that are necessary for productive legislation cannot emerge. Among the Democrats, things look no better. Here, too, the party is split into two wings: those who more strongly favor the centrist tradition of the Clintons versus the progressive wing that would have preferred Bernie Sanders as their presidential candidate. At the moment, the Trump phenomenon puts these dimensions of the crisis in the shadows.

Interestingly compared to Obama, under whom the blockade of the political system was still discussed as a central dimension of the crisis of the system, many commentators nowadays are quite glad to see the mechanisms of "checks and balances" function, because it has put the brakes on most of Trump's initiatives. Donald Trump's decision to circumvent the separation of powers by invoking a national emergency in order to fund one of his main campaign promises—the wall on the Mexican border—is a sign that this resistance is deteriorating and that his presidency will have lasting detrimental effects on the functioning of democratic institutions.

After only a short while in office, Trump appeared isolated, focusing almost exclusively on the base of core followers who had made his election possible. His electoral victory is the expression of a crisis that affects most Western democracies on both sides of the Atlantic. Compared to recent political developments in Europe, Trump's election was accompanied by such visible political and social consequences because in the United States a number of mechanisms that could have dampened the crisis are only weakly developed. Americans' general mistrust of government as a regulative authority, along with the strong focus on individual responsibility and market mechanisms, allowed the crisis of globalization to strike American society and its citizens in an almost unchecked way. The distribution of income and wealth is highly unequal in the United States, and the changes in the labor market also struck the unregulated sector powerfully. Exceptionalism? Yes, certainly in the forms it took, but not substantively. Europe, too, is deeply embroiled in the crisis of democracy.

Europe Disunited

"The old, fragmented Europe has given way to a European Union made up of twenty-five nations and 450 million citizens. It has more people, more wealth, and more votes on every international body than the United States. It eschews military force but offers guaranteed health care and free university educations. And the new 'United States of Europe' is determined to be a superpower, whether America likes it or not."[1] These are not the words of some crazy sage who has spent the last few decades living in a cave, cut off from the external world. Nor do they come from the obscure blog of a lonely fanatic. This is the jacket text of a *New York Times* best seller by journalist T. R. Reid, in 2004. Reid, in his book *The United States of Europe*, imagined the emergence of a "European colossus" that would threaten America's preeminence.

As remote as it now appears, in the middle of the decade that followed the millennium, this vision seemed thoroughly realistic. The European Union, in the midst of its eastward expansion, was about to incorporate twelve additional members. Its Lisbon Strategy was intended to raise pan-European competitiveness in the era of the "knowledge society." And economists confirm a massive economic boom during these years. After the dot-com economic bust had been overcome, the European Union's gross domestic product doubled.[2] Unity seemed within reach. Arguments about consolidation or expansion of the European Union were primarily academic and had little practical influence. People just kept floating along, buoyed by the wave of the euphoric 1990s. It seemed that the economically liberal Third Way was bringing with it political integration beyond national borders. The almost jealous gaze from the other side of the Atlantic, as conveyed compellingly in Reid's book, gives us an idea of what could have been.

A mere five years later, the optimism of the millennium had swiftly and completely evaporated following the eruption of the crisis. Talk of a colossus with global ambitions was nowhere to be found. The financial crisis split the European Union and then, during the years after 2010, morphed into the Eurozone crisis. The inequality between the northern countries and their southern, Mediterranean neighbors became ever greater—and massively skewed the European project. In the south, today, youth unemployment rates remain at more than 50 percent. In the north, especially in Germany, for the first time in fifty years, there are full tills and debates about where best to invest the country's tax surpluses—accompanied by growing social and economic inequality.

Even before the crisis, in 2007, British historian Timothy Garton Ash was writing very thought provokingly, on the occasion of the fiftieth anniversary of the Treaty of Rome: "Europe has lost the plot. . . . Europeans now have little idea where we're coming from; nor do we share a vision of where we want to go."[3] After the financial crisis, this lack of unifying ideas, of a common political project, became the most severe test the Union had yet had to face. Living together in a community driven by necessity rather than intentionality prevents solidarity between north and south. Moreover, and even worse, Europe, over the course of the last few years, has increasingly been made the scapegoat for the crises in individual countries.

The dissatisfaction was expressed first on the left. Podemos, Syriza, and the European antiglobalist movement Blockupy wanted above all to deal with the outgrowths of finance capitalism and the banking crisis. With the Arab Spring, the Spanish anti-austerity movement Indignados, and the global Occupy movement, it seemed that a global social movement for more democracy was coming together.

Brexit was a first manifestation of the right-wing nationalist fury against the establishment. Too much money, people thought, was being paid to the overcompensated bureaucrats in Brussels, while the same people were being deprived of control over their own politics and borders. The crass differences in voting patterns between city and countryside also show very quickly whom the protesters were targeting in the referendum on leaving the European Union: the leadership circles in London and their networks on the top floors and in the power centers of Europe.

The protest against inequalities, disconnected elites, and globalization was intensified by the refugee crisis. In the south of Europe, streams of refugees were coming ashore in E.U. member states Italy and Greece, which were still being buffeted by the effects of the financial crisis and where the problem of inequality was still worsening. In Germany, Angela Merkel's decision to take in nearly a million refugees was perceived by right-wing circles as treasonous and undemocratic. The Alternative for Germany attracted massive numbers of new members and saw more and more people voting for its candidates in local and regional elections, while in the summer of 2015, during the months after Merkel's decision, her popularity declined by 20 percent.[4]

At that time, especially in the German east, there was hardly a public event at which then-President Joachim Gauck or Chancellor Angela Merkel was not vilified as a traitor and the news outlets were not attacked as fake media. In Germany, the division of society that we can observe in various European contexts was especially pronounced. In Munich, hundreds of people welcomed refugees at train stations, and throughout the country, hundreds of thousands volunteered to make refugees welcome under the most difficult of circumstances. On the other side, there were those who denounced every gesture of opening as a denial of reality and who, in the most extreme cases, were setting refugee homes on fire almost every night.

In other countries, such as France, the neonationalists' displeasure was no less directed at the establishment. Le Pen was the clear loser in the final round of the election for president, but none of the big, established parties even got that far. The traditional political forces had been tossed out of the race, allowing Emmanuel Macron and his En Marche! movement to emerge victorious in the second round of voting. Soon after, the movement renamed itself La République en Marche! It was a conscious decision to avoid the idea of being a "party," while placing its bets on a social movement that seeks to overthrow the status quo and break up ossified structures.

Many people interpreted the result of the election in France as a defeat for the right-wing populists, which it certainly was. Trump's behavior in the White House, as president, surely also played an important role in deterring voters from supporting populists in France. But, overall, the French presidential election, just like Trump's, stands for the crisis of the political establishment, which no one any longer trusts to come up with a politics that can unite societies, reduce inequalities, and offer a perspective for the future. Meanwhile, given the pan-ideological protests of the yellow vests (*gilets jaunes*), Macron seems to be regarded as part of the establishment as well—foreshadowing problems to come. This is the common element that strikes the eye in most of the European countries: mistrust of the established parties, whose politics no longer appears convincing. As young voters and many minorities stay home during elections, the fringe parties on the right and left grow stronger.

The cause of this crisis of European democracies is also, and primarily, the politics of no alternatives as we have already sketched it out—not, for example, the crisis of state indebtedness, or xenophobia, or terrorism, all of which have intensified the crisis of democracy but did not create it. This is important, not least of all because it is also on the basis of this insight that the most urgent counterstrategy can be developed. For the moment, the historic window for a political vision for Europe, like the one that existed a long time ago, seems to be closing. If, however, the European Union remains an exclusively economic project, we are unquestionably only at the beginning of an even deeper crisis.

In Europe, the crisis takes a different form than it does in the United States, with a different force and direction. Right-wing populist parties are mobilizing effectively in the north and west of Europe. They succeeded with Brexit, too, in Great Britain, but until now are not in a position to win national elections there. Left-wing populists are leading governments in the European south. These two tendencies share a critique of Europe, but it is a critique with completely different contents.

The right-wing populists in the north want to go back to the nation and the nation-state; they want out of the European Union. They want to stop the process of European integration—even economic integration. The left-wing populists in the south (with the notable exception of Italy) want to create a stronger political project in Europe, one that goes beyond purely economic integration. They are demanding a more just Europe, and they want to give processes of globalization a social dimension. Right-wing populists are much weaker in Europe's southern countries, no doubt because the memory of authoritarian regimes is still much more vivid there. In Greece, Spain, and Portugal, the struggle for democracy was successful only in the 1970s. Georgios Papadopoulos, Francisco Franco, and António de Oliveira Salazar are still present in people's minds and thus make successful right-wing mobilization more difficult.

In Eastern Europe, the crisis of democracy is falling on much more fertile ground. There, traditions of a democratic order are much weaker. The transition from socialism to capitalist democracy that followed the fall of the Berlin Wall arrived in the form of a crash course. The politics of no alternatives was introduced with a pneumatic drill, propped up economically and politically, and sweetened with the promise of economic growth and European integration. When this promise could not be fulfilled, political mobilization from the right was a piece of cake.

In Europe, in other words, we find a very different sounding board for the politics of no alternatives. Hence the results also look different. They are framed by the process of European integration, which in certain respects intensifies the crisis but simultaneously attenuates it in others. The process of European integration, which is primarily economic, has led to inequalities within and among the European countries and thus plays a causal role in the growing crisis of trust in all European societies. At the same time, however, Brussels functions as a lightning rod in some member states. Guilt and responsibility are shifted from the nation-states to the European level as a means of legitimating national politics. The crisis of democracy in Europe varies by region, whereby the dual crisis—at both the nation-state and the European level—brings with it the dual dangers of deepening inequalities and a potential failure of the European project.

Europe's Historical Peculiarities

Actually, Europe's development is a surprise. In the relevant literature, the countries of Europe are seen as coordinated market economies with corporatist structures in which large firms partner with labor unions and the government. Collective labor agreements and a minimum of redistribution stand behind macroeconomic stability and social peace. Generally, therefore, Europeans are also considered more inclined toward state intervention than are Americans. The entire literature on "American exceptionalism" also speaks to this development. In Europe, in the late nineteenth century, the working class was more success-ful in integrating its interests within the political system. Social democratic parties have been solidly anchored in the political architecture of European democracy and func-tion as a transmission belt. Social policies emerged that were more strongly oriented to social conciliation. Thus, the state took on the role of moderator between capital and labor and derived legitimacy from this role. The result was the development of a state that is both social and interven-tionist, where "big government"—very differently from the United States—has not been considered a problem. Given our explanation of the crisis in the U.S., wouldn't we expect such a context crisis-proof? Odd, isn't it?

What is even odder: since the financial crisis, there has been a remarkable role reversal between Europe and the United States. Europe, with its significantly stronger tradition of the welfare state, turned to austerity politics in the hope that it would be able to save its way out of the crisis. In the United States, in contrast, Barack Obama's administration, after taking the reins of power at a time of economic free fall, decided in favor of government inter-vention and countermeasures. The land of liberal market economy called in Keynes, while in Europe, the home of social democracy, politicians rooted for austerity. A world turned upside down?

This contradiction actually says a lot about the final impact of the crisis of democracy. The tradition of the wel-fare state is indeed stronger in Europe. Some people see this as borne out by the significance of the nation-state in European history, where it is closely associated with both the hopes of the Enlightenment and the dangers of

totalitarianism.[5] The centralized state is a European invention. Perhaps for this reason, when it comes to redistribution and social justice, people there have more faith in it
than they do in the United States, despite Europeans' historical experiences of fascism. Even today, the different
historical paths to modern development taken by the European nation-states and the United States can still explain
some of the differences between the democracies on the
two sides of the Atlantic. How distinct is the European context? And how can we explain the paradox of today's crisis?

European Wonders and Their Undoing

Hans-Jürgen Puhle sees the different developmental path-
ways as determined by nationally specific mixtures and
developmental sequences in relation to three factors:
bureaucratization, industrialization, and democratization.[6]
Each nation-state, he argues, entered modernity with a specific bundle of the three factors, and this, in his opinion,
makes it possible to explain their unique features and the
differences among them. For instance, in Great Britain,
based on the dominant influence of a powerful and autonomous economic bourgeoisie, Puhle sees capitalist industrialization as the clearly leading factor driving the processes
of democratization and state authority and control. The
process of bureaucratization began only later, basically in
the second half of the nineteenth century, in order to overcome the consequences of industrialization. In the countries of continental Europe, by contrast, whose bourgeoisies
were considerably weaker, he finds different sequences and
combinations. There, bureaucratization was dominant,
in the form of bureaucratic absolutism, authoritarianism,

and militarism. In France, the French Revolution set the country on yet another path of development, with a combination of bureaucratization and democratization, while the process of industrialization took off only later and was essentially unable to put its stamp on French political institutions. No revolution like the one in France took place in Prussia and the other German states. There, as a result, a dominant mixture of bureaucratization and industrialization emerged, while the process of state control and democratization only finally set in after World War II.

Naturally, as the twentieth century continued, there were processes of convergence that started to play a role. This was reflected, first of all, in the strengthening of those elements within the triad of modernization factors that had been weakly developed in each case. But differences remained. The patterns of development that are found in the United States are, once again, unique, although more comparable to those in Great Britain. In contrast to Great Britain, however, the process of state formation and democratization in the United States was not driven solely by industrialization; it was present and dominant from the beginning. This has had consequences for the overall acceptance of governmental action in general and of state intervention in markets.

The European position, with its greater emphasis on state intervention, was further strengthened in the immediate postwar period, leading to a massive expansion of sociopolitical measures in almost all the member states. In France, the era of economic boom during the illustrious years after 1945 is referred to as *les trente glorieuses*, in Spain as the *milagro español*, and in Italy as the *miracolo economico italiano*. In Germany, too, the *Wirtschaftswunder* is deeply burned into the collective memory. It symbolized the turn toward the world and away from the total rule of the Nazis. The "economic miracle" is the birth date of the Bundesrepublik, when it reinvented itself as a social market economy that, rather than seeking more *Lebensraum* and eastward expansion, aimed to define itself as a pacifist and environmentally conscious nation that is on the way to exorcising its demons. Exemplary historical turning points in this reinvention of the nation include the 1968 student revolt against the parental generation and the 1989 reunification of Germany.

In the 1980s, the consolidation and expansion of European governments as interventionist and socially active states reached its high point. And yet expenditures kept rising. Thus, for example, the year 1990, according to OECD data, saw a public expenditure quota, that is, the sum total of government expenditures as a percentage of gross domestic product, of 42.6 percent in Germany. In 2010, it reached 47.3 percent. In some other European countries, the public expenditure quota even exceeded 50 percent. This was the case in the Netherlands (52.6 percent) and Sweden (56.2 percent). In the United States, during these years, the comparable quota was 37.4 percent—noticeably lower than the average among European countries, which was 48.1 percent. The differences between Europe and the United States are even more striking if we look at spending on social welfare. In Sweden, in 1990, social welfare spending accounted for slightly less than 30 percent of government spending; in Germany, it was nearly 22 percent. In the United States, in the same year, it was just above 15 percent.

But at the same time, during that decade, a change in direction was being signaled. Social democratic parties in

Great Britain and Germany, but also the Democratic Party in the United States, attempted to win elections again by making an ideological swerve toward the center. Free-market philosophy, developed in Britain and the United States and tested in the shock therapies that were administered in Eastern Europe after the fall of the Berlin Wall, were characteristic of the thinking of this new, pragmatic center, which we have already discussed at some length in an earlier chapter.

Around the millennium, in Germany, under the administration of Gerhard Schroeder, the social welfare state was restructured. The Hartz IV reform, which reduced social benefits for individuals who were unemployed for more than a year, and Agenda 2010, which lowered taxes along with medical, social, and unemployment benefits, are the main signposts that mark the end of the Great Promise in Germany. Many other European countries, after the fall of the Wall, also implemented market-oriented reforms that they hoped would strengthen their economies' international competitiveness. "Workfare" was the dominant slogan. Especially in the realm of social welfare, restructuring was aimed at creating stimuli for returning to work. The state was meant to activate welfare recipients and help them reintegrate into the labor market.

Exactly as in the United States, in Europe these reforms were also presented as being without any alternative—if, that is, the country wanted to continue to succeed in the context of global economic competition. In Europe, too, the reforms were not without sometimes contradictory consequences. Yes, in many countries income inequalities grew, sometimes drastically, as they did in the United States, and somewhat more moderately in other countries.

But interestingly this did not lead to a reduction in social welfare expenditures. On the contrary, in Germany, between 1990 and 2016, social welfare spending grew by more than 3 percentage points, while in the United States, during the same period, such spending actually declined by 6 percentage points. This shows that the logic of social policy has shifted, namely, from a concept of social citizenship to one oriented to activation and the shifting of responsibility to individual citizens. While this was justified by referring to the efficiency of the market, it now becomes clear that in spite of all the reforms the costs have increased. Perhaps pseudo markets create an even bigger bureaucracy when public goods are concerned?

On the whole, similar reform logics can thus be observed on both sides of the Atlantic. The United States, however, started with a comparatively much lower level of state-supported social welfare, while, at the same time, America's dominant liberal tradition made the country much more susceptible to the politics of neoliberal restructuring. In Europe, the tradition of socially oriented politics is much stronger. Even the reforms of the Third Way were not immediately able to consign this tradition to the dustbin of history.

Compared with the United States, the E.U. member states continue to evince a notably strong trust in government, which is expected to intervene by providing public goods and regulating markets. Naturally, there are differences among them, for example, if we compare Italy with Poland or France with Germany. Still, overall, it is possible to speak of a tradition of social citizenship, which has had a considerably more pronounced impact within Europe's institutional landscape—including in the minds of its citizens—than has ever been true of the United States. This tradition had the effect of acting as a brake on neoliberal reform politics in many European countries.

Where does this leave us? The crux of the matter, which also explains the above-mentioned paradox of the quite different and contradictory responses to the financial crisis, can be found in the disjunction between the nation-states and the European supranational state. The reason why Europe reacted to the crisis with austerity rather than state intervention was—as could have been expected in light of the institutional history—the fact that the European Union, unlike the nation-states, has no real European citizenry, much less a European *social* citizenship. The economic institutions of the European Union, such as the European Central Bank (ECB) or the euro, are not accompanied by any solidarity-creating political project. So while German finance minister Wolfgang Schäuble was imposing harsh austerity on Greece and the European south, Germany was simultaneously putting together social welfare packages and subventions for people to work reduced hours. While Greece was allowed to avoid bankruptcy and the ECB parceled out further credits under the strictest possible terms, the authorities were simultaneously ensuring that the creditors in the north did not have to incur any losses. The apparent contradiction, when it came to managing the crisis, shows above all that there is no political solidarity between the individual European nations—and hence that we are indeed looking at a dual crisis: one at the level of the nation-states, and one at the supranational scale.

Chapter 4

Crisis Dimension #1: Europe's Birth Defect

In the heyday of social welfare states after the end of
World War II, increases in production on both sides of
the Atlantic were linked to improvements in wages in very
much the same way. In the United States, a compromise
between government, capital, and wage workers resulted
in redistribution along the lines of Keynesian and Fordist
theories. The goal of state capitalism in Europe was also
to stabilize demand; the idea of social citizenship played a
role there as well. A reduction in inequalities was achieved
through transfer and tax policies accompanied by social
measures and by state intervention in the labor and financial markets—although in the Europen context women
and minorities participated less strongly in the postwar
boom than they did in the United States. The Great Promises of the postwar era brought increased social mobility
to the European countries, as redistribution and public
educational institutions began to break down the boundaries of class. In the 1950s, German sociologist Helmut
Schelsky even spoke about a "leveled-out" middle-class
society. Naturally, class boundaries did not disappear, but
at least there was an "elevator effect" that allowed everyone to share in the economic boom.[7]

But these sociopolitical achievements, which were
achieved in different degrees in individual European countries, do not carry over to the European Union. On the
contrary, many people actually blame their failure on the
European project, especially those who find it politically
opportune to do so. Citizenship in Europe's individual
nation-states is linked to different nationalities. The fact
that the promise of solidarity was made in the national

context of the individual member states rather than the supranational European entity also explains the nostalgia for the time before Europe.

All this is related above all to the social coldness that was a birth defect of Europe. Naturally, the main motivation was never again to want to see war on European territory. Only a cynic could claim that this was not meant seriously. Still, it was economic integration on which Europe's construction relied from the outset. This is true of the European Coal and Steel Community, also known as the Montanunion, which was founded in 1951, and also of the European Economic Community, which built on the Montanunion and was formed in 1957. The renamed European Community, which was created in 1993 by the Treaty of Maastricht and from which the European Union eventually emerged, was meant to place political questions, as well as economics, at the forefront of supranational cooperation. But in 2009, when the Treaty of Lisbon dissolved the European Convention and the European Union became a legal entity, the political dimension still mainly existed on paper. In reality, this moment marked the beginning of a stretch of history that had little to do with solidarity and social cohesion.

Very few people would actually speak of European citizenship. There is no European identity, no founding myth or myths, no European imaginary, no pan-European social glue. The liberalism that exists in Europe is thus purely economic—a liberalism that is concerned with efficient economies and trade and with political integration as the markets' collateral damage. It all has less and less to do with the political idea of Europe, which, let us not forget, could actually be traced back to the Enlightenment and early thinkers of political liberalism, such as Kant, Tocqueville, and Mill. The 1990s boom and the euphoria that accompanied the fall of the Iron Curtain allowed the European Union to ignore this shortcoming, although surveys from the period show that the lack of democracy was beginning to be strongly criticized even then.[8] This critique, though, echoed hollowly, given the distance that people already felt between themselves and the apparatus of the Union.

Crisis Dimension #2: National Reforms

Europe's democratic deficit was further deepened by a crisis within its member states, resulting in two long-term tendencies that together prepared the ground for the crisis of democracy. These problems within individual nation-states had been gathering force for some time, as in Europe, too, the 1970s marked the beginning of the end of the postwar project. The balance of power between employees and employers was shifting in favor of business. According to data gathered by the United Nations' International Labor Organization and the OECD, the rate of union membership declined in several developed countries of the transatlantic space. In the United States, the change, once again, was extreme: membership rates fell from 26.9 percent in the 1970s to only 14.8 percent at the beginning of the twenty-first century. In Germany, union membership also declined during this period, but far less sharply, from 32.9 percent to 29.1 percent.

There are exceptions to this broader trend. Rates of union membership remain very high in the Scandinavian countries, which have even seen increases since the 1970s: in Denmark from 61.3 percent to 76.6 percent and in Sweden from 66.4 percent to 85.9 percent. Here, it is necessary to take into account that in Sweden and Denmark the unions offer their members voluntary union-based unemployment insurance. This so-called *Genter-system* naturally serves as an enormous stimulus for workers to join the union, for only as a member of a union can a worker claim benefits under the unemployment system.

Nonetheless, along with the decline in labor union membership in the United States and many continental European countries, the transformation into so-called postindustrial societies was fraught with very serious consequences for employees across the board. Productivity increases were no longer passed on in the form of wage increases, especially not in industries (such as the service sector) where the unions had less influence. At the same time, big corporations were becoming more mobile and able to exert political influence. The expansion of the low-wage sector was massively encouraged, especially since the 1990s and, not only in Germany, led to a long and heated debate. The flexibilization and deregulation of labor and financial markets were also progressing. Part-time work, an important contributor to income inequality, grew from 11 percent to 16 percent when averaged across all OECD countries. It was especially pronounced in Germany, Ireland, Holland, and Spain.[9]

It is important to stress that it was not the structural reform of the labor market that set off Germany's economic turnaround in the mid-2000s. Nor was it the above-mentioned Hartz IV welfare reforms that resulted in growth. The decline in wages that made Germany more competitive had already begun a decade earlier and was a result of German unification and German automobile companies' penetration of foreign markets. Political scientist Mark Blyth therefore concludes, "The only thing the

Hartz IV reforms brought us was the creation of a very low-paid and not very productive service sector, which was not exposed to international competition and contributed to a drastic increase in social inequality in Germany."[10] Along with this comes the fact that not every country can be Germany. The boom in Germany derived from the country's ability, unlike its most important European trading partners, to use its ability to produce more and cheaper goods to put itself in a strong competitive position. But exports, by definition, also require corresponding import markets. Not everyone can be the export champion of the world. There also need to be world import champions. This is why Germany's criticism of its E.U. partners seems hypocritical, for without their readiness to import, Germany would not be doing so well today.

Although they never make it altogether clear what the causal relations are, its opponents hold the European Union responsible for the gradual tailing off of the postwar economic boom. Thus, it is not only that the social dimension was lacking at the level of Europe: Europe, as such, is also regarded as being partly responsible for the end of the era of welfare states. To many people, the European Union looks like a bureaucratic apparatus that busies itself with unimportant matters, such as the acceptable curve of bananas or the height of stair risers. It also appears as the gateway to a globalization that is no longer steered by politicians and certainly not at all by citizens, but by colorless technocrats who sit behind closed doors in faraway Brussels and ignore the will of the continent's peoples while they negotiate obscure free-trade treaties and special agreements with transatlantic corporations. The "Troika," which refers to the cooperation of the European Commission, International Monetary Fund, and European Central Bank, is perhaps the best known and most pertinent symbol of this technocratic rule.

With the restructuring of social welfare and labor markets, inequalities have also greatly increased, both within and among E.U. member states.[11] This trend grew by leaps and bounds after the fall of the Berlin Wall and especially over the course of the 2008 financial crisis. Even the economic recovery, which began around 2012, has not lessened the unequal distribution of income. In Great Britain, as in the United States, this trend is especially pronounced.[12] In Germany, whose economy, at the moment, looks best among the E.U. states, it is sometimes forgotten that just a short while ago people were talking about Germany as the "sick man of Europe." And, in fact, Germany's good unemployment numbers were bought at a high price: by the expansion of low-wage work, the acceptance of the inequalities within the European Union, and the reform of the social welfare state following the imposition of Agenda 2010.

Despite this parallel development of depoliticization at the European level and within individual countries, before 2009 economies were still growing and unemployment rates were still falling in almost all the E.U. countries. Even if these statistics were mainly based on the growth of the low-wage sectors, they made many people forget the actual problems. The crisis smoldered. The financial crisis was the first clear caesura, and it had very different consequences for Europe's individual member states. In this sense, the crisis of democracy was initially a creeping process in Europe, too. It developed in tandem with the restructuring of social welfare states, which created the first cracks in the relationships among E.U. member countries.

Chapter 4

With the financial crisis, suddenly, a wedge was driven between the continent's nation-states. In Europe, this led to a rift between north and south; some people would even say between Germany and the rest of the European Union. The financial crisis, itself a consequence of blind faith in the market, can be regarded as a trigger point for the current crisis of democracy. It made what remained of the idea of Europe after the fall of the Wall vulnerable to attack and reduced the political idea that once led to the creation of Europe to an economic skeleton.

One-Two Punch: The Financial and Eurozone Crises

In the summer of 2007, two of Bear Stearns's hedge funds, which had gotten into trouble, dragged some German provincial banks down with them into the abyss—German banks that had made bad bets on the U.S. mortgage market. In the United States, in the months leading up to October, one financial firm after the other collapsed. In February 2008, Congress approved a recovery package in the amount of $150 billion. In Germany, at this point, only the regional banks had been affected and were the butt of much spiteful commentary. But when Lehman Brothers went bankrupt in September, Merrill Lynch had to be bought up by the Bank of America, and the Dow Jones index experienced its greatest drop on a single day since September 11, 2001, it was finally quite clear that this was going to be a global crisis. The financial markets were too tightly networked, especially between Europe and the United States. By the end of September, the German federal government had jumped in with credit guarantees for Munich-based Hypo Real Estate Holding AG. One rescue package followed another: €480 billion from the federal government in October, plus additional measures and action plans designed to protect savings accounts and "system-relevant" financial institutions at the level of the European Union and the German federal states. The ECB repeatedly lowered its prime rate.[13]

A massive failure on the executive floors of European banking houses became a public problem for Europe, as the costs of the crisis were passed on to the populations, step by step. And not without chutzpah. As just one example, Commerzbank—whose chair, Martin Blessing, had admitted in October that the banks, including his own, had "truly not covered themselves with glory"—stepped forward the very next month, inspired by the Dresdner Bank's low stock price, to take it over at half price.[14] This is the very same Commerzbank that only a few years later, in 2015, was convicted of systematically aiding and abetting tax evasion and got off with a fine of only €17.1 million.[15] There are many more such examples—and at least as many attempts to reassure us that these are just a few black sheep in the banking sector, and that the problem is not greed or the character of certain professional groups but the incentive structure in this particular business sector. If this were changed, the problem would be quickly solved: this was the tenor of a whole stream of behavioral economic attempts to explain the crisis out of existence.[16]

But the rescue attempts, at taxpayer expense, left a bitter aftertaste. Was there really no alternative? Where, suddenly, did all the money come from after decades of pleading for building schools or repairing roads and being told that the government's coffers were empty? In Europe, at least, there was hardly time to give much thought to who the guilty parties were, for the financial crisis was quickly followed by the Eurozone crisis. More precisely, the question of guilt was not just postponed; it was reinterpreted. Suddenly, it was not the financial elites who were in the crosshairs of criticism but governments, which had simply taken on too much debt—especially other governments and their populations, for example, the "lazy Greeks." Far better to do as the "Swabian housewife" does and pay more attention to saving! This was the mantra of German finance minister Schäuble and Chancellor Merkel. In the midst of this determination of guilt, there was a subtle shift in the discourse— one that would have serious consequences. Suddenly, the financial crisis turned into a government debt crisis.

The Invention of the Government Debt Crisis

The financial crisis could have served as a warning sign when it came to liberal economic dogmas. Wasn't neoliberalism done for? France's president Nicolas Sarkozy suddenly presented himself as a critic of neoliberalism and called for a new debate on wealth and sustainability. Even Alan Greenspan, the former chair of the Federal Reserve, admitted before Congress in October 2008 that he had "found a flaw" in the model.[17] And the International Monetary Fund, infamous as the instrument of the Washington consensus's economic elites and known for its solidly market-friendly orientation, thought better of it and has since called for a reversal of financial policy and for combating inequalities. In the years following the crisis, the OECD ordered three large studies that provide details of the causes and consequences of growing inequalities. *Growing Unequal? Income Distribution and Poverty in OECD Countries* (2008), *Divided We Stand: Why Inequality*

Keeps Rising (2011), and *In It Together: Why Less Inequality Benefits All* (2013) are the three pointed titles of these influential research projects.[18]

For the European Union, the crisis might also have signaled a turn away from market thinking. Instead, it did just the opposite. It raised the politics of no alternatives—and along with it, frustration over the status quo—to new heights. Behind this was a historical revisionism that, almost unnoticed, reinterpreted recent history in a radical way. Instead of a crisis of the private sector, which is what the financial crisis was, in the European context, people were suddenly talking about a government debt crisis, as if the financial crisis were just an amplifier of a government crisis that had been long in the making. The banking crisis was perfidiously reinterpreted as a crisis of the public sector, making it possible to push market thinking and the politics of no alternatives even harder. With the reference to inordinately high government debt, the austerity politics and the undermining of the social welfare state that had occurred during recent decades were driven to new extremes.

Let us take a minute to savor this. Billions of public monies were spent to save "system-relevant" banks—"too big to fail"—from collapsing. Instead of rethinking the politics that led to the crisis, the explosion of government indebtedness that followed was used as an excuse for cutting back government welfare programs even further. This is astonishing—and astonishingly brazen. It can hardly be repeated often enough: the austerity policies are not a response to a government debt crisis but to a crisis (or crises) in the private sector.

Interesting, in this connection, was the apparently politically opportune change of heart of the political elites.

Government debt before this had not been a problem at all! In some countries, government debt as a percentage of gross domestic product was already at today's levels ten years *before* the crisis. No one seemed to take an interest in this, and yet today reducing government debt is being held up as the only way out of the crisis. We may be allowed to interject a question at this point: given the "close cooperation" between politics and economics, at the expense of civil society, is it surprising that a problem of legitimacy should crop up?

One final time: the government debt that has ballooned in recent years is, in fact, not the cause but the consequence of a crisis that began in the banking sector. The greatest crisis since the world economic crisis of 1929 was instrumentalized in Europe by various interest groups in order to advance their own agenda. This agenda is ancient and has proven that it does not deliver what it promises. A look at the past reveals how explosive this is. Mark Blyth may have come up with the most eloquent example when he draws parallels between the current crisis in the Eurozone and the world economic crisis of 1929, framing it in terms of another grave problem, namely, the gold standard. According to his argument, austerity politics is not a cure but a palliative for the government and for democracy.[19] It is not new, in Germany or elsewhere, nor was it necessarily the only possible reaction to the crisis.

Austerity politics is the belief that it is possible to save one's way out of crises. It is based on the fallacy that saving is always a virtue. But something that might be valid for an individual is irresponsible at the level of the state: governments sometimes have to incur debts to get out of crises. But defenders of austerity insist, even during a recession, that people have been living above their means and need to tighten their belts. In the 1930s, when Keynes called for anticyclical investment and redistribution as means to overcome the world economic crisis, people already knew that saving does not work. The answer was precisely *not* sitting it out and saving, as Joseph Schumpeter and Friedrich August von Hayek, the thought leaders of neoliberalism, wanted.

Blyth sees a fateful similarity between Europe then and now. The unbroken dominance of the idea of saving, especially in Germany, is one aspect of this. There are also similar institutional contexts. In the 1920s, the currencies of European governments were pegged to the gold standard. As a result, they had no ability to pursue their own fiscal and monetary policies. The connection to gold meant that the only means available to governments that were attempting to balance their budgets was deflation. Unemployment and wage reductions were accepted by elites as means of maintaining a dysfunctional system at the cost of society as a whole. The same problem exists in Europe today. True, there is no more gold standard, but in its place there is the euro, which functions in a very similar way. Today, too, European governments no longer own any money printing presses. The power to decide these matters is lodged in a European institution that is not democratically legitimated (which may sound familiar): it is the European Central Bank.

Current austerity policies include a defined repertoire of political-economic measures: budget cuts, wage decreases, debt reduction—in short, fiscal discipline, with the goal of balancing the federal budget. In fact, it also recalls the savings policy and methods pursued in the early 1930s by German chancellor Heinrich Brüning, with catastrophic consequences for the Weimar Republic and the

German history that followed—something that economics Nobel Prize laureate Paul Krugman emphasized and criticized quite soon after the outbreak of the crisis in 2008.[20]

In the 1920s and 1930s, austerity policy also seemed to the economic and political elites of many countries to be unavoidable. They accepted the frequently drastic social consequences as a necessary evil. Today, we see a similar picture: to salvage an ideological project, the European economies have risked a radicalism that is extremely worrisome for society. We have begun to see the consequences of this orientation in the last few years.

The Crisis in Europe Deepens

The reframing of the financial crisis as a government debt crisis and the forced imposition of austerity in Europe have led to a further deepening of economic disparities, beginning with the second decade of the current century. It has also led to animosity between countries. Actually, no one in Europe was even talking about a democratic deficit any longer, since this would have meant, minimally, that there had to be an idea of a shared European goal—which there was not. Within countries, the liberal-economic austerity agenda was reinforced internally. The restructuring of social welfare systems led to drastic increases in inequalities, along lines that in many countries traced the boundaries between rural-industrial and urban-postindustrial regions.

But the inner-European contradictions were also growing more acute.[21] A report by the emergency aid and development organization Oxfam Germany came to a telling conclusion regarding the inequality resulting from the financial and euro crises. The study confirmed, among other things, that "rich individuals, businesses, and private interest groups control the decision-making process in politics. The result: Tax systems and governmental policies benefit a few, but not the majority, which is why income and wealth inequality are rising." Along with this lack of responsiveness, the study concludes that it is not just that only a few benefit but also that many others have to shoulder the ensuing costs: "In some E.U. countries the costs of the austerity policies during the financial and economic crisis were borne entirely by the poorest. Under pressure from lenders, minimum wages had to be lowered, employee protections against dismissal done away with, and public sector expenditures cut back. In Spain, Portugal, and Greece, union negotiations at the national level were replaced by negotiations at the company level." And finally, inequality, which was already rising, was further exacerbated by "unjust tax systems" that "tax labor and consumption higher than capital," allowing "wealthy individuals, high earners, and big businesses to avoid their tax obligations. Thus, Spain receives 90 percent of its tax receipts from labor, income taxes, and taxes on consumption; taxes on business make up only two percent of income. At the same time, the E.U. countries lose a total of a billion Euros a year to tax avoidance."[22]

Jörn Kalinski, the head of advocacy and campaigns at Oxfam Germany, emphasizes that austerity would by no means have been without alternatives, and he suggests some ways out of the crisis: "Globally, the EU is a group of rich countries, but here, too, a quarter of the population is threatened by poverty. This is not an inevitable fate, but the consequence of a politics that has gone wrong and can be changed. There are alternatives: We can stop accepting poverty, inequality, and the political dominance of rich elites. For they threaten the social cohesion of our societies, and eventually democracy. We need more money for public services, tax systems that benefit the poor and not the rich, and standards for fair wages and working conditions."[23]

Within the German government, however, officials evidently do not want to take notice of the problem of poverty. There have been numerous accusations of censorship, fraud, and sugarcoating of results in the poverty report—and not without a public uproar.[24] In other European countries, the crisis is even more pronounced. Greece was forced by the Troika to sell off its crown jewels (harbors, airports, and so on) to be able to pay its debts to creditors in the north. Was there no corruption in Greece before the crisis? The question may come up at this point, as a way to justify the severe austerity measures. Yes, certainly there was. Nevertheless, the question is whether, in the long run, Europe can survive if the south is robbed of its future development opportunities and the vitality of its economies is nipped in the bud by draconian punishments. That the hope of an economic recovery in the Mediterranean region is slim is shown by the numbers of young people who are moving to Germany, where they hope to have a brighter future.

The midterm evaluation of the crisis is sobering. The financial crisis sharply exacerbated the already existing problem of European unevenness. After the financial crisis, economic disparities increased *within* E.U. countries.[25] In two-thirds of E.U. member states, the sudden increase in unemployment was the main culprit behind ever-increasing levels of income inequality.[26] Alongside these developments within individual member countries, the gap *between* rich and poor regions also widened. According to a study by the *Economist,* in the years before the crisis, regional divergences decreased, only to grow significantly after 2008. The reasons, according to the authors of the study, are to be found—along with deindustrialization—in an overvalued euro, low public expenditures, cuts in social welfare spending, and a rapid 6 percent decrease in the number of public employees. Since then, the decrease has been particularly devastating in already structurally weak regions of Europe, for example, Calabria and Slovakia.[27]

In addition to the geographic inequalities within and among member states, there is also a generational dimension that is reflected in the crisis of democracy today. Young people in the European south, above all, face a lack of jobs and future perspectives. They are also the ones who, in many elections and referendums, may not necessarily have been actively opposed to Europe, but during elections often stayed away out of feelings of resignation, making the ascent of the populists possible. There are too few possibilities to identify with the European project. The fact that Europe was conceived as an economic and not a political project does not entail only an identity problem, however. The economic dimension itself is in danger because the rigid institutional structures of European economic politics are misaligned with the unequal European zone.

Dissatisfaction Spreads

As more recent election results indicate, dissatisfaction with democracy correlates closely with educational level and social position. Members of the middle class and those with higher levels of education are more satisfied with democracy, both in their own country and, to an even greater extent, when it comes to the European Union.[28] Those who benefit from globalization do not necessarily see a crisis at all. Overall, however, there is a profound loss of trust. Suspicion of the political class within a person's own country is surpassed only by mistrust of the European elites. Member states shift the blame for their problems onto Europe and engage in European politics with their own population— not a common European project—in mind. There is a loss of trust both in the European institutions and in other E.U. members, which ultimately seem to be just as self-interested.

Approval numbers for the European Union already suffered steep losses following the financial crisis of 2008. In the fall of 2009, when Europeans still thought the crisis could be contained in the United States, Eurobarometer data showed 48 percent of Europeans as having a positive view of the European Union. Less than three years later, that number was only 30 percent. On the other side, the proportion of those who, over the same period, held a negative view of the European Union nearly doubled, from 15 to 29 percent. The highest approval ratings for membership in the Union by residents of member countries were registered in the euphoric years immediately following the fall of the Berlin Wall (71 percent in autumn 1990). Since the millennium, only every second person, on average, still sees his or her country's membership in the European Union as a good thing.[29]

Overall, the plummeting rate of approval for the Union is clearly associated with a population's own economic situation. Accordingly, dissatisfaction in the south is especially high among those who have been hardest hit by the economic crisis and is widespread except in

Germany and Scandinavia. Even before the refugee crisis, in the spring of 2015, in France, Spain, and Poland only about 40 percent of respondents reported feelings of trust in the European project. In Great Britain, the percentage dipped as low as 28 percent. And in Italy, a country that traditionally had a high level of enthusiasm for Europe, with approval ratings that at one time reached 70 percent, trust in Europe was recorded at 27 percent.[30] Enthusiasm for the European Union was already not high in the 2000s. Now it has reached a new low.

Refugees and Terrorism

No matter how you feel about Angela Merkel's decision to open the borders, one thing is striking: the structure of this decision, too, was top down, just as decisions were during the financial crisis and within the overall tradition of no-alternatives politics. The lack of democratic legitimation for a decision of such far-reaching import gave grounds for dissatisfaction. But perhaps even more important was people's fear of their own loss of position, stoked by forty years of neoliberal policies toward public social support and the labor market. Many people saw a reserve army of potential competitors in the low-wage sector, plus an additional expense item in the national budget, as affecting their own situation, especially in those regions of Germany that were structurally weak. That there was money available for refugees did not make sense to very many people: after all, they were supposed to be saving! It was a criticism that, notably, had been much more muted when it came to financial firms that cost the German government a lot more.

Along with this latent fear of a loss of status, which also affected population groups that could not be considered right-wing extremists, came a xenophobia that must not be overlooked. In Germany, given its history, national pride is a tricky subject. But it has been extensively dealt with, for which reason many people in the middle of society welcomed the burgeoning feeling of national honor that began to be felt after the World Cup in 2006. But the wish for this to be an open and cosmopolitan patriotism seems less and less realistic. Precisely in those regions where, after the fall of the Wall, people felt left in the lurch and blooming landscapes failed to appear, an exclusive, xenophobic nationalism has arisen and—in the most literal sense of the word—lit a fire under the refugee crisis.

In Dresden, there began to be weekly demonstrations by the far-right group Pegida (Patriotic Europeans Against the Islamization of the Occident). These soon attracted imitators in other places. People started—thereby distorting history—to suggest a connection to the liberation movements that had arisen during East Germany's peaceful revolution. The demonstrations became mass events. Encouraged by the agitated, flag-waving mood, some groups evidently felt emboldened to carry out, in 2016 alone, nearly one thousand attacks on refugee shelters, often including unapologetic threats to human life. But it was not just the East. As early as October 17, 2015, there was an attack on the city of Cologne's deputy for social welfare, integration, and environment, Henrietta Reker, whose agency was responsible for, among other things, housing refugees.

To this explosive cocktail were added the first terror attacks to take place in Germany. Political attempts to prevent the debate over terrorism from becoming linked to the refugee issue had limited success, partly owing to the fact that some terrorists had in fact used the refugee route for their travel to Germany. This allowed them to divide European societies even more effectively. The fear of terror also fueled right-wing nationalist circles in other parts of Europe and even beyond Europe, where Trump attempted to win points with massive criticisms of Chancellor Merkel. The image of a society under threat from all sides was employed in the Netherlands, France, Austria, and elsewhere as a way to mobilize against immigration and revive old nationalist reflexes. There were different versions, to be sure—for example, in France, the Netherlands, and Great Britain, where entire colonial histories still resonate—but they always had the goal of stirring up and expanding the group's own base.

If the criticism of the financial and European crises had previously been coming from the left (for example, Podemos and Blockupy), by 2016, at the latest, the wind was shifting. Criticism of neoliberalism became a critique not of economic liberalism but of the political ideals of the liberal model of democracy instead. Under attack, multiculturalism came to be seen as the root of all evils in an alienated society. The critique of the elites was still there but under a different sign. Anyone who disagreed was accused of refusing to recognize reality and of being a goody-goody or a traitor. Those elites, extremist circles claimed, wanted to "exchange" the *Volk*, to replace it by bringing in foreigners and handing people's pay and bread over to less demanding citizens. It was a new, more extreme version of the old story: "Outsiders are taking our jobs away."

But even apart from this, in the course of 2016, the refugee crisis became a problem for Europe. After the financial and economic crises had already created a deep split, the response to the influx of refugees threatened to dissolve altogether what was left of European cohesion. The Dublin Regulation, which was agreed to in 2013 and provides that in most circumstances individuals seeking asylum in Europe must apply to the member country through which they first entered the European Union, made Italy and Greece the de facto reception centers for refugees. Hungary, Poland, and the Czech Republic closed their borders completely, in spite of the threat of fines, and in other countries many refugees are interned under very harsh conditions and kept away from the public.[31] The situation is rife with potential future tensions.

While the combination of a terror crisis and a refugee crisis have brought the right-wing extremists out of the woodwork and into action within individual countries, an icy tone of mutual accusation characterizes communications between the nation-states, as they attempt to foist the burdens of the crisis onto their neighbors. Italy and Greece, which had already emerged damaged from the earlier economic crises, have been especially hard hit. The north-south disparity is mirrored here, as is the corresponding crisis of democracy. While criticism of the European Union has clearly grown, with few exceptions, the degree of satisfaction with democracy inside individual countries varies. Here, too, the divide runs between north and south. Especially in Greece, Croatia, and Hungary, the last five years have seen significant increases in dissatisfaction.[32]

To strengthen political communities, what is needed are either external lines of demarcation or shared successes. In the European Union, in recent years, the trend to draw lines between members has become increasingly prominent, while talk of successes has not been frequent. But perhaps the confidence of the 1990s can be reestablished? To be sure, in response to the above-described threats, civil society actually has begun to position itself. However, unlike the years immediately after the fall of the Wall, the new confidence will have to be drawn not from economic but from political integration if its supporters do not want to fall into permanent crisis mode.

Europe as a Political Project

Where do we stand today? In comparison to the rest of Europe, Germany does not seem to be in such bad shape at the moment. Unemployment is lower than it has been in years; some people even talk of full employment. Germany still claims top honors as export master, government debt seems to have decelerated, and even the poll numbers for the Alternative for Germany are stagnating, in some *Länder* (German subnational states) actually declining. And yet, Germany seems far from having overcome the crisis of democracy—and the Alternative for Germany's numbers are still remarkably high. While, in comparison to its neighbors to the south, Germany seems to be doing relatively well in terms of the raw economic statistics, the large, traditional parties are still in an uproar. Election results on the subnational level have been devastating for the Christian Democrats and even more so for the Social Democrats. What is more, German economic stability has come at the price of European destabilization.

The impression of Germany as an "Isle of the Blessed" is deceptive. Neighboring countries bear the brunt of its export surpluses. In light of these current account imbalances, the haughtiness with which Germany lords it over the other European member states seems rather hypocritical. The debts of some are the surpluses of the others. Then there is the situation inside Germany itself, which we discussed above. Since the 1990s, the low-wage sector has been massively expanded. While in 1995 the share of this sector among jobholders still stood at 17.7 percent, by the beginning of the financial crisis it had risen to 24.2 percent. In other words, in Germany today, nearly every fourth employed person works in the low-wage sector and thus earns less than €10 per hour. Many population sectors have seen no income increases since the fall of the Berlin Wall. The fruits of increased productivity have not been equally distributed: most of them have gone to those who already had plenty.

Thus, even though Germany's economy is once again growing, export records are broken every year, and the unemployment numbers are low, many Germans justifiably do not trust these positive statistics. The impression of stability seems to come primarily from the contrast between Germany's relative well-being and the volatility in the international arena. The person who today earns only low wages, and each year receives a report projecting his anticipated income in old age, will spend many a sleepless night thinking about the problem of poverty among the elderly. Already today, according to data from the federal government, the average monthly social security payment to a single individual in Germany is only €1,366. For some 10 percent of single pensioners, social security pays no more than €500 to €750 a month to that person's account—this at a time of rising housing costs and rent indexing. In big cities, such as Munich, Frankfurt, or Hamburg, it is barely possible to survive on this. Approximately 15 percent of people older than sixty-five years of age are at risk of poverty. If we look only at individuals with lower educational qualifications, the percentage is still higher, at 25 percent.

In Europe overall, the crisis is even more complex and has already passed through several phases. At the time of the changes that took place around 2010, the lack of solidarity among countries helped encourage social movements that were politically left. Since then, however, it has been mainly the collective fear of an external threat that has helped movements and parties on the right end of the political spectrum find new dynamism and win elections.

In the American context, we located the cause of the crisis of democracy in the depoliticization that accompanied economic liberalization, as it unfolded beginning in the late 1970s. Economic liberalization further hollowed out a public welfare state that was already quite meager, leading to economic inequalities that made the status quo and the politics of the establishment no longer tolerable. There can only be social cohesion in an unequal society if upward mobility seems possible, especially if, as in the United States, inequalities are being rationalized based on opportunities for advancement. The financial crisis, the high indebtedness of students and households, and the social exclusivity of the superrich have all contributed to making the American dream of success and upward mobility increasingly unlikely, while politics seems to have lost its connection to the concerns of citizens, and responsiveness has become a question of purchasing power.

In Europe, we see a similar picture. It is painted in the same colors, but because of the way the state is structured, it is more multilayered and complex. For one thing, the European Union's member states have developed very different social welfare institutions and political systems. Each of these national contexts embarked on its own different Third Way. As a result, every crisis follows a different, institutionally shaped path, so Germany's crisis of democracy looks very different from that of Greece or France. For another thing, the individual states have very different relations with each other, which also partly explains the malaise that affects the European project. The crisis of the European Union is made up of several individual crises, which are mutually reinforcing. Over and above this, there exists an enormous tension between the European framework, with its regulatory and monetary-policy instruments, and the web of relations among very unequal member countries with sometimes conflicting interests. This mismatch was clearly made more acute during the financial and Greek crises. It has also found expression in disagreements over immigration and security policies, and it holds the medium-term, certainly not inconsiderable danger that the European project may fail.

The more general crisis of the European Union has long been described as a crisis of democratic deficit. In that sense, it is nothing new. What we found in the United States is even more acute in Europe. Whereas in the United States specific political ideals and democratic institutions have been hollowed out, in the European context they never actually existed or existed only at the national level. This birth defect of European democracy confronts the Union as a whole with a challenge that may tear it apart. And these longer-term, European-level tendencies toward crisis are being further exacerbated by national and international dynamics and tensions.

In Greece, the alternative to no alternatives is called Syriza; in France, National Rally. Thus, instead of *a* crisis of democracy, we are compelled to speak of *several* crises. And yet, despite all the variants, we can see how in the European context the political ideas of liberalism are being undermined by economic interests. Here, too, the crisis of democracy is an immanent crisis of liberalism. The question is whether the stability of individual countries can hold the historic project of a union together.

It is not yet possible to predict how the crisis of democracy in Europe will end. Optimists can point to the tradition of the social welfare state and the relatively less severe inequalities (at least in the north) compared with the United States. One could also cite the defeats of right-wing candidates in France and the Netherlands. Perhaps, after all, the Europeans have learned their lessons of the world wars?

Those people who tend toward skepticism have equally convincing arguments. They point to the unacceptable economic differences between north and south or to youth unemployment around the Mediterranean. But the fact is that the individual interests of the nation-states do not seem to coincide with the interests of Europe as a whole and its corresponding institutional structure; this is the decisive reason why the crisis of democracy in Europe must be addressed as a primary concern. Overcoming these particularisms will require a concerted, new dynamism by democratic forces and European civil societies—and will demand nothing less than a new vision of the common good.

Chapter 5

The Beginning of History

If it is true that the market ideology of the Third Way and the politics of no alternatives have led to a crisis of depoliticization, it would nevertheless be wrong to think that as a result politics is no longer important. On the contrary, the depoliticization of the public sphere, which has often been chastised as political apathy, seems to be turning around since Trump's election, resulting in a strongly political moment. The U.S. midterm elections have brought new debates about how to tackle economic disparities and climate change, and the Democratic Party has entered an important process of renewal. In Europe, people are joining political parties, demonstrating in the streets, and deliberating political issues. The European Union has launched multiple campaigns to engage its citizenry—and seems to be hitting a nerve, with young voters in particular. Technocratic economic liberalism is politics, too, but now, once again, people seem interested in thinking about whom it serves. Even if it sometimes gets overshadowed by political spectacle and populist rhetoric, the trend is worldwide.

If we define politics as goal-directed activity, the question arises as to who formulates the goals. Experts? Companies? Politicians? At the G20 meeting in Hamburg, in July 2017, rage at the elites spewed forth again. For many, the divided TV screen was telling. It contrasted the visit of state leaders to the Elbe Philharmonic, on one side, with the street battles in Hamburg's Schanzenviertel, on the other. With all the talk of violent confrontations between police and demonstrators, all the images of burning cars—which unlike the burning refugee hostels caused great indignation and led to demands for a strong response from the German police and judiciary—the political issues at stake were completely pushed into the background. The pent-up anger that is vented in the yellow-vest movement in France bears a similar risk of crowding out politics through a media focus on spectacle and violence.

But the urgent questions do not just go away. What must democracy look like in the twenty-first century? How is it possible to have more equality without negatively affecting freedom? Is democracy even possible against the background of growing climate crises and resource shortages? If we think back to the unbroken series of crisis scenarios of the last few years, the situation does not augur well for a rethinking of politics. Politics is always also hope—hope that something different can be done. But it must be made clear against what or for what politics articulates its goals. Which crisis (given the admittedly great choice among crises) is the one we should most urgently address?

Instead of focusing on the crisis of democracy, some commentators are referring to an antiliberal revolt or a restoration by the enemies of democracy.[1] They insouciantly throw Brexit and Trumpism in the same pot with the rise of Recep Tayyip Erdogan, Viktor Orbán, and Vladimir Putin, and argue that the critique of elites is unjustified and that the various forms of neonationalism are a chauvinist reaction to liberal democracies, multiculturalism, and open societies. This interpretation misses the point and is intentionally misleading. It cynically distracts from the actual problem of Western democracies in order to hold onto the old tendency of a politics of no alternatives. To represent the critics of globalization as enemies of democracy, as these neoliberal apologists do, is dishonest, especially when the proponents of this view instrumentalize democracy in order to profit personally from globalization at other people's expense.

In the transatlantic context, what we see is not merely some irrational plot against democracy. It is a movement that runs counter to the economic and social politics of the most recent decades, which has used the ideas of an open society and cosmopolitanism solely as a means of masking the economic interests of those at the top and painting them in pretty, humanistic colors. Establishment forces still take cover behind the same values, which by now have lost their power to convince. Because multiculturalism and political transparency have been misused as a fig leaf for the expansion of markets, these politically liberal projects have gone up in flames. These days, the political ideas of liberal society seem to be no more than deceptive maneuvers. But instead of rethinking them in new ways, many politicians continue to use them to follow the old script of liberalization and deregulation.

Emmanuel Macron's victory in the French presidential election of 2017 was valorized by many people as a triumph of democracy, although it must have been clear to most observers that a vote for him was merely a vote against Marine Le Pen. After only a few weeks in office and as the result of a politics, once elected, from which only the rich stood to gain, many people had already turned away from the new savior. The yellow-vest movement made it clear to observers that support for Macron seems frail and that his labor market reforms are stoking the flames rather than rallying the people. What this philosophy of staying the course and "business as usual" means politically, in the longer term, should actually have become clear after Trump's election. Even the most unpopular candidate of all time, with a clear narcissistic personality disorder and a not very attractive ego, was able to win out over the candidate of the status quo because he mobilized disgruntled voters in old manufacturing regions and because minorities and young people did not turn out to vote. But instead of learning from their mistakes, the parties of the center on both sides of the Atlantic are mostly behaving as if, as an alternative to neoliberalism, nothing exists but the fallback into fascism and dictatorship. This crude clinging to the politics of no alternatives will further consolidate the crisis of democracy.

Why the Crisis Is Not over Yet

Certainly, we could also paint a completely different picture of the situation. Was Trump really that successful? Will he actually leave much of an imprint on U.S. society after he leaves office? Despite the dominance of the Republican Party in both houses of Congress and on the Supreme Court, he was not able, during the first half of his first term, to impose his power as strongly as some people had feared. Most legislative projects, except for his tax reform, failed. Trump primarily governed by executive order, which means that a Democratic president could rather easily overturn his policy initiatives—in much the same way that Trump sought to undo his predecessor's legacy. The 2018 midterm elections signaled the rise of a young, diverse, and ambitious political force within the Democratic Party, which might soon help to unseat him and reverse course. His escapades are gradually spelling doom for him, and some of his core supporters, suburban women and white educated men, seem to be turning away from him. Although his attempts to undo the separation of powers are cause for grave concern, they have mostly failed, at least for now. And so, perhaps, might Trumpism be overcome as quickly as it made its brief appearance on the world stage?

In Europe, too, the populist wave of 2016 seems to have lost some of its momentum. Macron clearly won the second round of voting, while Le Pen was left in the dust and had no chance. In the parliamentary elections for the Assemblée Nationale, Macron's victory was further consolidated, not least because his popularity, bolstered by strongly worded comments about Trump and Trump's climate policies, won him many new votes. In the early parliamentary elections that Theresa May called in June 2017, totally confident of a victory that would strengthen her own mandate, the prime minister had to accept a bitter defeat, while the Labour Party under Jeremy Corbyn, who was known for his leftist political positions, saw a clear increase in votes. The right-wing nationalist U.K. Independence Party—the party that Trump's protégé Nigel Farage had once headed—was unable to win a single seat in Parliament. Even the Alternative for Germany seems to have passed its zenith. In the Bavarian and Hessian elections in the fall of 2018, it captured only 10.2 percent and 13.1 percent of the vote, respectively, indicating that support seems to be leveling off. Moreover, internal struggles and a scandal surrounding illegal donations to the party from unknown sources in Switzerland and the Netherlands make it very clear that the party has fully arrived on the rocky terrain of political reality. Even though Merkel's days as a politician are numbered, and despite the fact that Macron is experiencing much more turbulent times than he did in the immediate aftermath of his election, democratic forces see a silver lining.

On the whole, voter participation is growing. In Great Britain, it is once again at 69 percent—not yet 78 percent, where it was in the 1990s, before the rise of the politics of no alternatives, but a whole 10 percent above the figure for 2001. Young people, too, seem to have recognized the seriousness of the situation and to be returning to the voting booths. This potential to remobilize whole groups of voters who had turned away will certainly be a deciding factor in overcoming the crisis. The wind actually does seem to be shifting. Even in the United States, where mistrust of government is very strong, more and more citizens are reacting to the inequalities and are increasingly prepared to welcome government intervention in market mechanisms.[2] After Trump's election, millions of women took to the streets to demonstrate for greater social justice.

The potential for overcoming the crisis is palpable. But it would be wrong to underestimate the existing dangers to democracy. The apparent awakening of citizens was, first of all, a choice between two evils. This does not in itself provide the foundation on which sustainable structures can be built. If the root of the problem is not addressed now, the crisis of democracy will become a chronic illness. If once again there is no departure from the script of no alternatives, the damage that has already been done will not be reversible.

We do not want to awaken false expectations. Ways out of the crisis of democracy in Europe and the United States will be laborious. Europe suffers from a deep divide between north and south; youth unemployment in the Mediterranean region is enormous; and the institutional rigidities of the E.U. apparatus make failure more likely than sudden triumph. If people do not unite quickly around shared political goals, the project of the European Union will soon be a thing of the past—not least because the instruments of political rule are in crass contradiction to the political facts on the ground. The interests of individual countries must be fitted into an effective federal structure in which the interests of citizens are more strongly represented, as well. This is the only way for the European Union to become legitimate and democratic.

The standing of the United States as the world's leading military, economic, and moral power has been badly damaged. The inspiration that this country long radiated has faded within an extremely short period—and with it the liberal vision of democratic peace through international institutions and global market integration. In the United States, Trump has done great harm to the country's democratic institutions. Trump's bungling maneuvers attacking the institutions of the separation of powers have further eroded trust in political life there. Behind the flak of his irresponsible administrative actions, the lobbyists of the oil and finance industries—invited into the government by Trump—have made sure that environmental and consumer protections, as well as the entire financial sector, have been massively deregulated. This makes the economy in the medium term more susceptible to crises and increases inequalities, while pouring oil on the fire of the political crisis. Trump's strategy for defense against Russia, regardless of how great his own guilt may be, definitively harms democracy by crudely disregarding the established mechanisms of checks and balances.

But although the crisis has not been overcome, it is not impossible to overcome it. We would like to remind readers that in Great Britain, the United States, France, and elsewhere, renationalization has always only been pushed by a minority. Hillary Clinton received about three million more votes than Trump. And more than ninety million people, approximately 40 percent of the eligible voters, did not even vote. This means that less than a third of eligible voters cast their ballot for Trump. His victory, consequently, was entirely dependent on the peculiarities of the American electoral system. As with the Brexit vote, it was above all the failure of young people and minorities to go to the polls that made the rise of the nationalists possible. In France and the Netherlands, the national forces actually failed. But if it was just a straw that broke the camel's back, then there is hope that future elections can expect more defensive actions by civil society. The early elections in Great Britain showed what happens when young people once again vote and do not turn away from politics in disillusionment.

When minorities went to the voting booths, they gave Barack Obama significant victories in the presidential elections of 2008 and 2012. These segments of the electorate must be mobilized if people want to stop the rise of the demagogues. And the 2018 midterm elections sent a strong sign that this is by no means impossible. Although Democrats did not take back the Senate, they won 69 percent of all Senate races. Their gains in the House of Representatives are the most decisive in a generation. The election will be remembered as the first congressional election in which Muslims were voted into office and the biggest cohort of women won seats on Capitol Hill. At the same time, it is worth noting that some of the most successful progressive candidates, notably Alexandria Ocasio-Cortez, had not even been the Democratic Party's first choice. In fact, Democrats tried to get established candidates elected instead. And so, while the Democratic Party did not exactly experience a surge—or a "blue wave," as it was called at the time—November 2018 was a moment of hope, despite the absence of a clear political vision and even against the Democratic Party's own will.

Nevertheless, repeated votes for the lesser evil will not be sufficient to chart the way out of the crisis. A consensus driven by the fear of even greater damage by demagogues would mean another descent into the next crisis. Given the differences in political context that we have presented in some detail above, it should be clear that there cannot be *the* golden path out of this predicament. But if the crises of liberal democracies are a result of the fact that economic interests and logics have hollowed out political systems and notions of value, then in principle the key must be to put politics back in the foreground—in front of the apparently invincible forces of globalization. Markets must serve societies, not vice versa. Politics, in turn, must offer a space where societies can negotiate decisions about which public goods they need, what it means to be a citizen, and which realms of life can be marketed.

By definition, everything that is inescapable restricts freedom of action; everything that seems inexorable leads to passivity and encourages acquiescence instead of a political response. So if a social development seems necessary and nonnegotiable, no political discussion of other social ideas and proposals and models can occur. If the crisis of democracy is a crisis of depoliticization, then its cause is to be found in the assumption that globalization is inevitable. This supposition lies behind the politics of no alternatives that links the crises on both sides of the Atlantic ideologically. To overcome this crisis, it will be necessary to reconquer politics and take it back, both theoretically and in practical ways, from the markets.

Political liberalism, which served to legitimate the economic politics of no alternatives, is equally available for a turn away from a market-centered type of globalization. The idea of an open and tolerant society will have to be reinvented if political communities want to hold onto this ideal, which has been one of enlightenment and emancipation. The problem—and the opportunity—will be that it is not possible to fall back on the language and fundamental assumptions of the politics of no alternatives. Accordingly, politics will have to be conceived once again as a good in itself and not as collateral damage of growing markets. To do this, we will need a new social contract governing political practice in which social relationships and fundamental assumptions will have to be renegotiated.

Chapter 5

One Single Crisis or Many Crises?

But is it, then, just *one* crisis, all the parts of which could at least in principle be approached similarly? The more closely we examine the details of the crises in Europe and the United States, the less plausible it seems, initially, to talk about one and the same crisis of democracy. In the United States, we see the long-term effects of the financial crisis, which delivered a sudden shock to a much-troubled social welfare structure and constantly growing inequalities—to such an extent that it actually drove the traditions of self-reliance and small government *ad absurdum*. Europe faces a dual crisis, with a democracy deficit at the European level that, as a result of restructuring during the Third Way, made political decision-making in the individual member countries more technocratic. The shock of the global financial crisis further eroded the already shaky cohesion between the nation-states—a problem that was drastically intensified by the European crisis and that after the refugee crisis took a right-wing nationalist turn. In Europe, with its many member states, the picture is especially complicated—an unresolved low-grade combat of all against all, with conflicts of interest between individual countries and at the interstate level.

And yet, as we have seen, despite the variety of political traditions and very different institutional landscapes, actors, and outgrowths of the individual crises, it is possible to reduce the crisis of democracy to similar developments: on both sides of the Atlantic, in the 1980s and 1990s, people turned to a market-oriented politics of no alternatives. To fight inflation and stabilize prices, social programs were cut back, the floodgates of international trade were thrown open, and financial markets were liberalized. Thus the problems of a growing social welfare state could be resolved in the sense of the one percent. Instead of full employment, the goal was the stability of wealth. Under these circumstances, companies could grow past the borders of individual countries and beyond the requirement to account for themselves at the national level. The compromise between government, capital, and working people, on which the postwar Great Promise of economic upward mobility and prosperity had been founded, was called off.

In the United States, because of its market-liberal social structure, the inequalities grew especially quickly. While lobbyists' influence on politics increased, responsiveness to the middle classes, which were becoming less cohesive, declined. At the same time, opportunities for upward mobility disappeared. Rising tuitions and growing inequality have turned social mobility—the anchor of the American dream and the social glue of the society—from an achievable utopia into a cynical commentary on the existing conditions. To this is added a heavily indebted group of young people who can no longer pay off their debts. This already tense situation was then hit, in the years 2007 and 2008, with the biggest financial crisis since the world economic crisis of the 1920s. This time, it was not only disadvantaged groups already affected by globalization— African Americans, Hispanics, and other minorities—who suffered but also those groups that had previously benefited from the era of Fordism. White workers, especially in the Rust Belt of the Northeast and Midwest, suddenly had to fear for their jobs and status and faced the threat of becoming debt-ridden or even homeless. Students, who at least had still counted on the possibility of their own

being imposed more and more often, justified by pointing to the lack of alternatives—until the ultimate, alternative-less scenario of the U.S. banking crisis overflowed into Europe, striking first the federal state banks and then all the big, massively overleveraged financial firms. The creeping crisis of a technocracy, at *both* the European *and* the individual country levels, became a galloping crisis that divided the continent along national lines and incited whole populations and state actors against each other. Into this explosive situation, in the fall of 2015, flowed the refugee streams from Syria and North Africa. The critique of economic liberalism was turned on its head, into a critique of the political values of liberal democracy. Suddenly, multiculturalism was the evil responsible for all of society's injustices.

If Trump is not the crisis but its symptom, then this is also true of the refugee debate. To bring stability and democracy back into the realm of the possible, it is necessary to get to the root of the liberated markets and market ideology. If public goods decline even further, while at the same time goods and benefits are only being redistributed upward—by means of tax cuts, continuing reductions in educational and health care benefits, and so forth—then there is no end of the crisis in sight. And this is not all. In this case, social peace is also endangered. Once things have reached this point, it will be difficult to live in the same prosperity and peace that only a short time ago people thought was self-evident.

The Need to Embed Markets

The progressive reforms that Karl Polanyi described so perspicaciously with an eye to the early twentieth century offered a possible release valve for channeling the opposition movement.[3] But today's societies are not necessarily compelled to respond to the undermining of their markets with progressive, reformist measures. On the contrary, the crisis can also become chronic. Trump himself has already mutated from a symptom to his own form of crisis. He has given the opposition movement in the American context a specific direction that can no longer be described as liberal. Even as it drives the neoliberal politics of privatization and deregulation to new heights, it is ultimately turning away, in neonationalist fashion, from the founding political ideas of the Third Way. This turn away from groupthink may entail dangers, but it also offers a chance—the chance to reinvent politics.

We have already explored the consequences of the rise of markets in detail. They include increasing inequalities, the concentration of wealth at the very top of societies, and a closeness between political and economic power that is becoming more and more problematic. The dominant ideas about the market and its virtues corresponded to the interests of these more elevated social strata—and were presented as a common-sense assumption that was literally unquestionable. Perhaps more invisibly, the fields of mainstream economics and the positivist social sciences contributed to this perception by reinforcing the idea that markets make up a separate realm that is independent of politics and society. Margaret Thatcher's quip that there is no such thing as society, only individual men and women and families, coincides with the short-sighted, economistic view of societies as the sum of individuals and their drives—completely separate from structures, historical contexts, and institutional settings.

But markets were always part of social relationships. They are embedded in society. Their failure is thus always also a social question. If, since the 1980s, people in the competitive states of the transatlantic world have begun to orient their own market economies to the global economy, this has not been without consequences for Western societies. Dancing to the tune of the markets has been disadvantageous for politics, since there no longer seemed to be any other option than going along with them. This sealed the doom of organized labor, whose unions and collective interests seemed to evaporate in the course of deindustrialization.

In sum, the immanent crisis of liberalism that we have described on both sides of the Atlantic is an expression of a restructuring of economic activity at the global level. It is a longer-term crisis that will also require longer-term solutions. There are some corrective measures that must be undertaken immediately and that vary in the United States and Europe since they correspond to specific functions of the respective political systems. However, there are also structural questions that cannot be solved in the context of the nation-state and have to be approached at a supranational level. The nation is one possible way out of the crisis, but it is dangerous—and renationalization will not suffice to solve the problems we face in the long term.

The Nation as a Community of Solidarity

As we have argued, not all the supporters of Trump and Brexit were right-wing extremists. And yet, the demagogues' rhetoric succeeded in mobilizing a sufficient number of votes. The reason this worked is surely that the idea

of the nation does not signify only racism and exclusion—
as Europeans, for historical reasons, have good reason to
believe. Instead, it offers a space for projecting and formulating the rights of groups and individuals, and it also
stands for solidarity and inclusion. The nation must not
necessarily be conceived as exclusive, as right-wing populists do, but has always also been an emancipatory concept
aimed at the integration of different groupings.

Enlightenment thinkers and early political liberals
already emphasized the importance of a feeling of belonging. In the late eighteenth century, Montesquieu invoked
the spirit of the laws, meaning the political community
that would have to form the basis of every political society
if it was to work. Early in the period of industrialization,
Tocqueville added that in the era of technology, markets
and rationalization did not suffice to make democracy
possible. Citizens had to learn to be democratic. A "religious spirit" and civil society were needed in the cities
in order to prevent social isolation, or the dissolution of
traditional families and village communities would lead
to individualization and ultimately to the breakdown of
the commonwealth. Industrialization and urbanization,
therefore, also meant an undermining of democracy.

In short, we need to believe certain things in common
in order to make democracy work. At the end of the nineteenth century, when the reform movements in Europe
and North America began, in opposition to the inequalities and social distortions of industrialization, Ernest
Renan emphasized the very same thing we mean when we
talk about the inclusive character of the nation. The human
being, he wrote, was "a slave neither of his race nor his language, nor of his religion, nor of the course of rivers nor of

the direction taken by mountain chains." The individual, as part of a nation, was not a member of an ethnic, much less a racial community, but rather a voluntary member of a "large-scale solidarity," to which the individual had to recommit him- or herself in a "daily plebiscite."[4]

A political community, in other words, is not just the sum of rational solitary combatants. This is not sufficient: social glue and a principle of community are required for a partnership of convenience to become a political community. The values of political—not economic—liberalism take precedence. These values do not have to be exclusive and xenophobic but can also construct a shared social project based on integrative traditions and values. In recent decades, we have seen the political dimension of social projects become less important. In the United States, the relationship between individual striving and the country's unity myths has become skewed. In Europe, at the supranational level, there is no social or political project worthy of the name, while, at the same time, individual member states no longer build on the idea of social citizenship. There will have to be a new kind of belonging if we want democracy to work.

The nation as an idea was essential in the nineteenth century. At the time, it produced the needed social cohesion and in doing so first made the economic development of industrialization even possible. It created a sense of community among newly emerging mass societies. It mediated between the cold calculation of the markets, the ahistorical bureaucracy, and the fates of individual human beings. As a social bond, it held together energies that were otherwise pulling apart. Communities were invented to counteract the centrifugal force of capitalism.

At the same time, of course, nations prepared the ground for the atrocities committed in the name of nationalism in the twentieth century, since internal integration can also be accompanied by external closure, especially when citizenship in the nation is based on ethnic criteria. Political identities are the object of fierce struggle because they are also associated with questions of status and access to public goods and government services.

As Craig Calhoun points out, "we should approach nationalism with critical attention to its limits, illusions, and potential for abuse, but we should not dismiss it."[5] Democracy requires political subjects. In the past, the nation was this political grouping; it synchronized the market and the state. It was possible for the nation's working people—who, at the same time, also constituted the collective, democratic "people"—together with its business owners and politicians, to forge a social pact that after the world wars would engender the Great Promises of the twentieth century. The story is well-known. The idea of social citizenship, which includes claims to social services for all citizens, was the central notion that allowed shared participation in politics. The decisive question in the context of the globalized markets of the twenty-first century is: how must this social pact be newly defined in order to make something similar possible? To what extent can we revert to the nation? And at what point does this become a problem?

National Strategies

In fact, there seem to be certain very pragmatic steps that can be taken at the level of the nation in order to beat a path out of the crisis, precisely because at the start of these reflections we must confront the question, who, after all, is this "we"? Who, in other words, may act legitimately as a political entity? Starting here, it is also possible to resituate responsibilities and mechanisms of accountability that actually correspond to what citizens are thinking. Thus, at the national level there are multiple possibilities to improve political processes and relegitimate democratic governments. They vary according to the specific context, but overall it will be a matter of using redistribution to improve chances for social advancement. Social cohesion can only return when people who earn less see possibilities for improving their life situation. At the moment, this is not sufficiently the case in either the European or the American context, which is why nostalgic references to the postwar period play into the hands of the Pied Pipers.

In the United States, two political realms seem especially important in this respect: education and health care. College tuitions have exploded since the 1970s. Many students no longer manage to pay off their loans and so become lifelong debtors. Bernie Sanders was especially successful in arousing the enthusiasm of young people because university reform took first place on his agenda. Loan forgiveness, better regulation of markets for student debt, and tuition reduction based on publicly funded alternatives must become important items on the political agenda if the narrative of social mobility is to become believable again. The health care system, for its part, affects an even larger part of society. The danger of falling into poverty owing to a lack of insurance is something many Americans are all too aware of. That social services are dependent on the condition of the labor market makes the U.S. population and its politics overly dependent on economic growth. Systems of social security must be decoupled from the market if people do not want to be faced with a new Trump after every economic crisis.

Europe, for its part, will have to be reinvented socially if there is going to be a European Union a decade from now. This means redistribution not only within individual countries but equally between the member states. The gap between north and south must be overcome, for it is the source of the division between individual countries. For this to occur, there will have to be a new way of approaching macroeconomic and fiscal policies that does not play the members off against one another. Some people argue in favor of the notion that a new shared security policy could become a unifying factor for the European Union.[6] Especially after Trump called on Europe to become responsible for its own defense, this seems like a plausible move. But it, too, is a very one-sided vision. A social solution is needed, one that fixes attention on the social problems and does not ground unity on militarism and fear of outsiders.

It is important to emphasize the following: the triumph of the European Union does not and cannot hinge on the failure of individual states. As the authors of a study funded by the Bertelsmann Foundation recently concluded, "the E.U. should offer a framework that combines openness and mobility with social cohesion at the domestic level. It should support some of the core functions of national welfare states at a systemic level, and it should give orientation to nation states in their material development by setting general social standards and establishing goals and ways to learn from one other, while leaving the means of doing so up to the member states."[7]

How is this to be accomplished, given market discipline, budgetary discipline, and governments' lack of efficiency? How easy it is to fall into the usual argumentative patterns. But possibilities actually do exist for putting the social welfare state back on its feet. Government budgets, like all budgets, are made up of income and expenditures. One can spend less—austerity—or take in more by increasing taxes, especially on the superrich. Tax havens must be shut down. That this is possible, if the political will is there, has been shown in Germany, for example, by the compact discs from Switzerland that made it possible to convict whole lists of tax cheats.

Beyond this, there are very concrete steps that can be tried in individual country contexts in order to restore trust in democratic institutions. In the process, Europe and the United States can definitely learn from each other. In America, redistricting is as big a problem as voting rights. To guarantee participation, voter registration in the United States must be simplified. The primary system is too opaque and fragmented to do justice to its actual purpose of ensuring that candidates are democratically chosen. The Electoral College is another institution that has outlived its usefulness; it presents a particularly big problem in times of polarization. Especially in the United States, it is essential that the influence of capital on the political system be reduced. Along with reforming the laws that regulate financial contributions to electoral campaigns, this also means instituting checks and balances when it comes to the influence of lobbying on the daily conduct of politics.

Conversely, Europe, especially Germany, can learn from the ideal of a civic nationality that prioritizes democratic institutions and civil participation, not ethnic background or geography.[8] From a European perspective, people sometimes chuckle at the low rates of voter participation in the United States. In individual member states of the E.U., there may still be reasons for this because voting turnout is significantly higher. When it comes to elections on the level of the European Union, on the other hand, Europeans have not yet done their own homework.

To this must be added new demands for accountability by nation-states. For quite some time, people have acted as if states were nothing more than agents of transnational economic actors. This picture is misleading. Although the relationship between the state and the market has shifted, and in fact the cooperation is often too close, the state was and remains the decisive actor in globalization. Its market-creating and market-preserving activities—for example, securing property rights, signing free-trade agreements, and subsidizing the economy by investing in infrastructure and education—must be acknowledged and critically interrogated.[9] If globalization without governments is an impossibility, are the interventions by governments then just? Who gains and who loses? What would a just society have to look like, and what can the state do to bring one about?

All these questions can be asked at the level of the nation-state—and in the case of the European Union also at the supranational level. We are talking about short-term solutions that could be carried out immediately in a span of a few years if the political will is there. A civic nationalism around core values and a common social project can help mobilize that will. But there are also longer-term projects, some of which cannot be undertaken only at the level of the nation-state. Certain challenges of the twenty-first century do in fact seem to transcend the sphere of action by nation-states and will require new political instruments if we do not want to wind up in a chronic crisis of democracy. For this reason, returning to the nation-state is only a partial solution.

A New Social Pact

Every era comes with its institutions. Thus, the modern idea of bourgeois-liberal democracies arose at a specific moment in history. Before that, there were already centralized states in Europe, thanks to the absolute rulers who sought to consolidate powers under their personal control. But actually modern nation-states were a nineteenth-century phenomenon. Industrialization contributed to the creation of a new public sphere that demanded rights to equality and freedom—precisely those rights that had been formulated during the Enlightenment, when the ability to convert them fully into reality did not exist. These political values could only mature in this very special context—namely, a moment when political, economic, and social forces were more or less in balance.

No rulers or politicians decided to offer the lower classes new rights based on a sudden insight. But with industrial labor, a new social stratum was able to establish itself in the cities, organize massively, and demand a piece of the social progress. This was only the case because entrepreneurs and industrial bosses were not immediately able to increase competition through alternate sources of labor. Offshoring work to foreign countries did not yet exist as a possibility, nor did the technology that would have been required. It was necessary to come to an agreement inside the borders of the nation. This laid the foundation for the compromise between the state, workers, and capital that we identified above as the starting point of the postwar period's Great Promises.

As the twentieth century dawned, however, supply chains and trade relations extended more and more beyond the national borders.[10] In the process, the political and territorial logic of the nation-state and the economically expansive dynamics of trade, which during the era of industrialization had still coincided, became incongruent.[11] Political and economic spaces, which since the rise of the bourgeoisie had been mutually supportive and thus enabled the rise of the working class and the creation of a middle class, no longer overlapped. The final break came in the 1970s. Among the long-term consequences of this break is today's crisis of democracy.

The emergence of global production networks meant that the coincidence of political and economic spaces disappeared again. As a result, labor unions and civil society also lost their grip on the economy. The balance between capital, workers, and the state, which as late as the mid-twentieth century still led to the redistribution of production increases and made possible the expansion of the welfare state, went awry. The service jobs that have emerged in the "postindustrial era," for their part, are often only poorly organized and are located in the low-wage sector. As we have seen, in both the United States and Europe, it is precisely these population groups, who had gained from the compromise and now feared downward mobility, that have swelled the ranks of the protest parties.

To overcome the crisis of democracy, new institutions are needed that correspond to the realities of the new economy and can oppose it successfully. The current inequalities are not sustainable, in terms of social peace if nothing else. The question is whether it will take civil war-like conditions to make redistribution once more potentially feasible.[12] If we look to the past, we will unfortunately be compelled to decide that the answer might be yes. But it is possible to learn from history, is it not?

An economically secure citizenry is required for democracy to be possible. For this, there must be a new social pact. This cannot be simply a matter of reversing globalization and renationalizing: that is already impossible based simply on the existing state of technology. Rather, what is needed is a more just distribution of the gains of globalization. Expressed somewhat differently, markets must once again be better embedded in societies. Markets should serve societies, not the other way around.

What is certain is that the path of exclusion and isolation that Trump and others have embarked on cannot be a lasting solution, not least because of such global problems as climate change, resource shortages, and forced migration. We are going to have to come together in a more powerful way, not just economically but above all politically. But if the crisis of democracy, at its core, can be said to have been caused by the lack of congruence between the spaces of political and economic action—and by the accompanying reallocation of power and resources among global commercial actors, the state, and citizens—then a new landscape of political institutions must emerge that corresponds to the new conditions of global production and consumption networks.

We need new ideas about citizenship and the rights and duties that go with it. The social citizenship of the Fordist era was national in its orientation. That made sense, too, based on the national nexus of mass consumption and production. In light of globalization, it would be more appropriate to consider *residential citizenship*. Social services could then be tied, no longer to national citizenship, but to a person's residency and place of work. This solution would do more justice to the reality of migration and the importance of global cities as the nexuses and control centers of international economic networks.[13] But, to be sure, it comes with its own risks of deepening the urban-rural divide.

With all these proposals, one might want to ask: how could all this be paid for? We have already mentioned tax-based redistribution and the shutting down of tax havens. A one-percent tax on billionaires, worldwide, according to figures provided by the United Nations, would flush $45 billion into public coffers. A tax on financial transactions has already been widely discussed, although since the financial crisis this debate has lost some of its dynamism. According to estimates developed by the European Parliament, a tax of this kind could generate $650 billion worldwide. Naomi Klein, who makes this calculation, also includes a tax on carbon and an end to fossil fuel subsidies, along with a reduction in military spending, all of which would bring in an additional $1.5 trillion. To this, naturally, can be added possible increases in corporate taxes and in individual income taxes on the superrich.[14]

Additional financing possibilities will be found. This will be necessary, too, for the social welfare state is built on the idea of national labor—something that in some regions no longer seems to exist in the traditional sense. According to a study by the Bertelsmann Foundation, by 2050, as a result of technological development unemployment in

Europe could grow to 21 percent and in North America to 26 percent.[15] A 2013 study by Oxford University predicted that in the United States, in the coming decades, progressive digitalization could lead to the loss of 47 percent of all jobs.[16] The utopia of the end of work is an old one. John Maynard Keynes, in the 1930s, thought the grandchildren of his generation would be mainly preoccupied with figuring out how to make sensible use of their leisure time. His vision of the fifteen-hour week did not materialize, however, presumably also because capitalism is always creating new possibilities for work—including actually unnecessary "bullshit jobs" in the financial and insurance industries, as David Graeber argues.[17] In any case, the distortions in the labor market have had important consequences for the organization of political communities.

The dual impact of these shifts is self-reinforcing: the future of work means increased costs for the social welfare state on one hand and a simultaneous decrease in tax revenue as the main source of income for its programs on the other. Experts who, based on these changes, believe it will be necessary to introduce an unconditional basic income are no longer in the minority. The decisive issue in this debate is whether a basic income completely replaces the social welfare state and only subsidizes the low-wage sector or whether it actually creates scope for development that also offers added political value for working people. Here, too, what is needed is a political, not an economic, debate over what kind of work should be shared and how.

Indeed, nearly everyone who currently makes prognoses about the future of work seems to be in agreement that these distortions are going to occur and that in a transformed nation-state governing will be different and

of participation are discussed, without giving the slightest thought to who is posing the questions that the user, from the comfort of his or her couch, is expected to answer in a "low-threshold" manner.[22] This technological optimism also stands behind the concept of the smart city, which is supposed to resolve all the problems of democracy in exactly the same way but never gets past the question of efficient resource allocation. Technical advances and technology can bring progress, but the political questions "What for?" and "For whom?" remain essential. All the TED talks in the world and all the "research" papers coming out of think tanks and industry do not diminish the urgency of these questions and the problems behind them. Quick technological fixes offer hope. But they also bring the danger of passing right over the actual political questions and covering them up, quite irrespective of the fact that they are solving problems that have yet to be created.[23]

Contours of a Global Federalism

The time has come to think more than just instrumentally. Certainly, reforms at the national level are important. But given the extent of the crisis, this is the moment for big changes. Above all, we want to start a discussion, not to propose a uniquely valid path to a solution. Debate itself is the politics that went missing in the era of no alternatives. These fundamental, partly utopian discussions must be flanked by short-term reforms of the kind we have already discussed, but there must also be deeper reflection that thinks beyond healing the symptoms. Certainly, the market has not been able to absolve us of all political decisions; it has only postponed them and made them invisible. We are not at the end of history, but we must learn how to think politically again.

We therefore want to put out a call for radically new thinking, first because we believe the technical means do exist for such a global political infrastructure. In the private sector, after all, it is possible to organize supply chains and production networks on a planetary basis over great distances. There also exist, in emergent form, global institutions such as the United Nations, which fail only because of the persistent power of the nation-states. Beyond this, already today, identities are more multilayered. We are not simply German or Spanish or American. We also define ourselves in accordance with our local and regional background and, yes, according to what unites us as human beings.

But we will have to rethink; it is unavoidable. Skeptics will have an easy time criticizing our proposals. How is something that does not function properly at the national level supposed to work globally? But to the person who dismisses all this as goody-goody-ism, we say: Perhaps we have no choice but political renewal. The migration that is going to be unleashed by climate change and resource scarcity cannot be dealt with at the symptomatic level, with new walls and border technologies. The streams of refugees of the last few years could be just a foretaste, if we cling to the same old national ways.

Anyone who thinks seriously about how we can bring political, economic, and social forces back into balance will rapidly return to the central question: Who should be the global subject that can act legitimately? Maybe it is the nation, after all? The polis in its contemporary form as the global city? Global institutions such as the United Nations? The question of the "we" is in fact not so easy to answer.

But who, then, says that all political questions should be resolved by one and the same political entity? In Germany and the United States, people are familiar with federalism, which has different responsibilities and jurisdictions for local communities, regional subnational states, and the central government. Unfortunately, this national federalism does not yet seem broadly enough conceived in light of such global problems as the climate crisis, terrorism, and inequalities. To really attack these crises in a way that is sustainable, there has to be a *global federalism*.

What might such a new political infrastructure look like? The decisive question will be the issue of democratic legitimation. Creating responsiveness and channels for advancement within nation-states is a crucial step. The same is true of other political spaces. It is not necessary to invoke the bogeyman of world government. *Horizontal* axes of cooperation can build on existing partnerships. Here, German-French relations can be cited as an example just as readily as global *Francophonie*. Missed opportunities are not lost opportunities. These existing networks should be built out and extended with a view, additionally, to such problem areas as the environment, infrastructure, and security. Partnerships between cities and regions, such as the C40 Cities Climate Leadership Group or the Clean Air Coalition, can also contribute.

One thing is certain: not everything must be negotiated and legitimated at the global level. *Vertical* axes of cooperation can also lend renewed legitimacy to political processes. What is decisive is the principle of *subsidiarity*: what can be carried out at lower organizational levels should be dealt with there. In this way, it is possible to imagine that responsibility for installing public infrastructure in cities is a job for urban and regional institutions, which must be appropriately accountable to their citizens. The same could apply, for example, to the organization of schools and educational institutions, transportation and communication, and hospitals and the whole infrastructure of health care. In matters of local government, Europe has a lot to learn from the United States, where more than 90,000 communities organize everything from fire departments and schools to pest control.

Of course, not all towns and cities are equally prosperous. There are often big differences in wealth between rural and urban areas, for example, between the densely populated city of Berlin and the more rural state of Brandenburg that surrounds it. This is one reason for the polarization of liberal democracies that we have been discussing. The tax income that is available to finance public infrastructure is very dependent on the residents' incomes—something that also occurs within cities. The problem is especially blatant when public infrastructure is no longer meant to be provided by the state but instead by the market, which is oriented to the purchasing power of potential customers and underserves less wealthy areas.[24] To confront this problem at a local level, it is necessary to cross-finance structurally poor and wealthy regions. Ultimately, everyone benefits from this kind of deconcentration of capital, which makes it possible, for example, to take away the sting of such phenomena as gentrification and rising rents—another subject for regulation at the local level. This sort of approach also works against the problems of segregation and ghettoization inside cities.

To achieve redistribution among regions admittedly will require political authorities at higher scales than local governments. It makes no sense to invest all our hopes in the era of urbanization and the participative possibilities afforded by cities, as the United Nations Human Settlement Program and many others have done, for example. Certainly, global cities and metropolitan regions are one possibility for achieving participation. But not all public goods are local. And the cities themselves are enmeshed in larger trade networks and relations.[25] As an example, the construction of the railways, highways, and electricity and communication grids that connect municipalities cannot be left to the market alone, since it has been proven that the market does not provide these kinds of public goods in sufficient quantity or in an efficient way. Here, too, *in between* metropolitan regions and cities, it is quite literally important not to be left behind. There is a strong connection between the supporters of right-wing nationalist parties and access to public transport systems: the more mobility and connectivity there is, the less nationalist the populace also seems to be. Here, too, cross-financing is essential. There must be coordination at the regional and national levels and mechanisms for accountability to the affected populations.

In recent decades, it has become quite usual to present public-private partnerships as especially efficient and financially effective—not least of all because government, after all, is meant to be small and to play second fiddle to the market. Yet there are thousands of examples of such partnerships and quasigovernmental institutions, such as port authorities and other semi-public agencies, that have not created the desired efficiency at all but instead have fallen prey to corruption, exploding costs, and a lack of transparency. Berlin's new airport is perhaps the best-known example in Germany, but there are many more. Something needs to change when it comes to the structure of these only half-public enterprises, which ordinarily mean that the companies cash in on the long-term profits while the taxpayers are stuck with the risks and ultimately with their costs. Here, too, there will have to be a debate about the necessity of public investments, and it must also be possible to ask the question which areas are really more efficiently served by the market when it comes to achieving a given objective.

All this is familiar, and all can still be managed at the local or national level. A more skeptical view of the market and new requirements for government spending would accomplish a lot. But economic networks, after all, are global, and to overcome this imbalance additional answers are needed at the international level. They cannot be delegated to small or subsidiary political institutions. International air transport, global stock markets, and international container shipping are examples of this.

Today, these economic fields function according to the principles of cost shifting and arbitrage. Their infrastructures and technologies serve as economic instruments for locating discrepancies in the political, legal, and labor conditions of different countries and taking advantage of this unevenness to reap a profit. Beyond this, states have reorganized institutions in such a way as to pass the cost of transportation and communication systems along to societies' weakest constituents. The wheels of trade want to be greased! This is the only way globalization can work! But the low cost of the transportation and communication that it takes to move jobs around the globe, to force deindustrialization, and to break up labor unions are not simply a consequence of technological innovation. It was nation-states that made these exchanges possible by means of massive subsidies for research and development; enormous investments in infrastructure and the deregulation of finance, transport, and communication networks; the nonregulation of labor rights and environmentally harmful actions; and by enacting free-trade agreements and providing investment guarantees.

These are all political decisions that were and are being made every day. They appear technical but have critically shaped the world in which we live and work. If they are being made by politicians, then there are also alternatives. Are these investments just? Does everyone benefit equally from them? Who gains from international trade? Who loses? In other words, the costs of globalization must be internalized; that is, they must not be fobbed off on the public and its weakest members but must be borne by those who profit from them, namely, such global actors as Ikea and Walmart, hedge funds and Goldman Sachs, Monsanto and Bayer.

Does this mean a planned economy? The person who asks this question is acting as if the market economy were not already being steered by governments. But this is how it is. The state may have become less visible, but it never went away. Since the 1970s, too, decisions have always been made about which companies to subsidize, which branches of industry to protect, which infrastructure to construct. But these decisions were not discussed among the broader public; they were made behind closed doors and with the excuse that there was no alternative.

One thing, therefore, is to make these processes transparent. Just recently, the German government publicly stated that it would not permit German companies to be bought up by non-Europeans if critical infrastructure is involved. Is this the beginning of a new way of thinking, or is Germany once again going its own way?

Until now, we have only been talking about infrastructures that have to do with trade and exchange, because they have the most direct impact on the inequalities. At the global level, there are naturally other urgent political realms that individual nation-states cannot get a grasp on by themselves. Various responsibilities in these areas, such as the climate crisis and terrorism, could be coordinated in different ways. The climate crisis is immediately linked to the trade issues that we have already begun to address. Here, uneven development is a critical point of concern because Europe and the United States, which were able to industrialize early, now want to make this same development difficult for other countries. Here too, solutions can only be found cooperatively. The example of terrorism has made it crystal clear that international institutions such as the Security Council have structural weaknesses that have to be addressed. The inequality embodied in its veto rights, for example, is a relic of the Bretton Woods era that preceded decolonization. It is Eurocentric and profoundly unjust and undemocratic. These institutions must be democratized if, in the long term, we want to get hold of the imbalances within the global system. Only by doing so will it be possible to democratize globalization in a way that will actually be global.

We Are What Is Needed

Although our proposals for a new political infrastructure may seem unachievable, a global federalism of the type we have sketched out would be altogether doable. The fact that today even this approach seems unrealistic or utopian is a reflection of the current interests of those who profit from the way society is currently organized. Partly, it is the economic and national elites, and partly it is we ourselves who (putting our own salaries at risk) enjoy cheap groceries and consumer goods manufactured by poorly paid workers. Some of us want to save money, others have to do this. But things could and can be different.

If we look to the past, we know that social change can indeed occur even when it seems impossible. What subject of a feudal lord would have thought he or she could one day be a citizen of a state? What slave in the United States in 1860 would have thought it possible that he or she would become free and equal? What woman, in the first half of the twentieth century, would have seen equality as an achievable goal? Progress is possible, and today it must be conceived globally. Otherwise, the populations of different countries will be played off against each other. And otherwise, the actual problems of the twenty-first century will remain beyond our ability to solve.

Reforming politics alone will not do the trick, however. The excessive power of the markets also needs to have a counterweight in the form of a strong civil society. State regulation is important at various levels, but *we ourselves* must also become active. This is true, for one thing, of our behavior as consumers. Markets, in theory, are responsive. If the Commerzbank, for example, systematically contributes to tax fraud, it must be punished by its customers—especially if the government is hesitating. If Deutsche Bank is doing billions of euros of business selling weapons and is speculating in foodstuffs, civil society must react. But the commercial enterprise must also undergo a profound change of heart. The idea that companies should simply pursue profits and then everything will be fine is just as wrong now as it was in the eighteenth century. Private firms' indifference to what is right is actually not to the advantage of the public. Why not see markets as realms of moral activity?

In addition, the institutions of civil society must be strengthened. Despite their weaknesses, political parties have demonstrated their value when it comes to transforming collective interests into policies. At the moment, admittedly, many people in Europe and North America have lost their trust in political parties.[26] To overcome the lack of responsiveness in representative systems, in particular, what is needed are strong parties that are able to reflect a multiplicity of political interests. Improving the organization of civil society also means that labor unions must regain influence. They do not have to be the industrial unions of Fordism. But there is nothing that in principle prevents workers in the service sector, for example, from organizing more effectively. This requires political will and civic engagement. Social movements are not some cliché left over from 1968. Political matters must be renegotiated over and over again.

A functioning democracy also needs a strong public sphere, in other words, media outlets that live up to their role as the fourth estate and watchdog—and that simultaneously provide citizens with the information they need. Could we institute a new inspection system for media like the one that exists for automobiles—a system that tests minimal qualitative standards and can restore public trust? Citizens themselves must also possess the competencies appropriate for democratic participation. This presupposes a minimum of education and civic interest. Universities will have to rethink their increasingly single-minded orientation to the labor market if they are to contribute once again to education that is relevant to participation in the public realm.[27]

Many questions arise when the end of history is at an end. They are questions that point to problems of civil society and political institutions. Do we need universal/ global, national, or macroregional solutions? Should we emphasize reform scenarios that are geared to specific aspects of politics? How can decisions be democratically legitimated? How can we make global federalism a reality? What practical intermediate steps can we take on the way there? Can norms be established globally and implemented at the level of individual states? What knowledge do we need? What kind of citizens should we become? How does social mobility work at the global level?

Civil society is readying itself, and the debate is already well under way. Overall, it seems clear: not everything can be directly legitimated. But via subsidiarity (decision-making that is done at the most local level possible) and differing federal structures for different aspects of politics, accountability mechanisms and institutional structures can be created that recapture globalization politically. In the process, new technologies may play a decisive role. For example, social media could serve as forums for participation (rather than for destructive accusations spewed out by trolls) if providers ensured the credentials of contributors. Citizens will require competencies and resources—and the corresponding social-welfare state infrastructures.

For now, it is not the technical details that will determine the outcome; it is political will. If the political will exists, then globalization no longer appears to us as an insuperable external force but instead as something that can be shaped. Only then can the crisis of democracy be overcome. With this, we would be standing not at the end of history but at a new beginning.

Notes

Chapter 1

1. Whitehouse.gov, "The Inaugural Address: Remarks of Donald J. Trump," January 17, 2017, accessed December 21, 2018, https://www.whitehouse.gov/briefings-statements/the-inaugural-address.

2. Quote translated from German. "Der Brexit war der erste Stein, der aus der Mauer brach," *Die Welt*, July 12, 2016, https://www.welt.de/politik/ausland/article160071342/Der-Brexit-war-der-erste-Stein-der-aus-der-Mauer-brach.html.

3. Quote translated from German. Maria Fiedler, "Europas Rechtspopulisten wählen Trump zum Vorbild," *Der Tagesspiegel*, January 21, 2017, www.tagesspiegel.de/politik/enf-treffen-in-koblenz-europas-rechtspopulisten-waehlen-trump-zum-vorbild/19286384.html.

4. Quote translated from German. "Petry fordert 'den Mut, Europa neu zu denken,'" *Frankfurter Allgemeine*, January 21, 2017, http://www.faz.net/aktuell/politik/inland/europaeische-rechtspopulisten-treffen-sich-in-koblenz-14715719.html.

5. "Europas Rechtspopulisten."

6. Bernie Sanders, *Our Revolution: A Future to Believe In* (London: Profile, 2016).

7. Naomi Klein, *The Shock Doctrine: The Rise of Disaster Capitalism* (London: Picador, 2008).

8. See for instance, in the German language, Ralf Fücks, *Freiheit Verteidigen: Wie wir den Kampf um die offene Gesellschaft gewinnen* (Munich: Carl Hanser, 2017).

9. How differently economic restructuring has affected different parts of the population is impressively documented by the work that Ruth Wilson Gilmore has published on California. See *Golden Gulag: Prisons, Surplus, Crisis, and Opposition in Globalizing California* (Berkeley: University of California Press, 2007).

10. Wendy Brown offers a brilliant analysis of this "economization" of politics in *Undoing the Demos: Neoliberalism's Stealth Revolution* (Brooklyn, NY: Zone, 2015). In *The Knowledge Corruptors: Hidden Consequences of the Financial Takeover of Public Life* (Cambridge, MA: Polity, 2015), Colin Crouch highlights a similar predicament.

Chapter 2

1. University of Virginia, Miller Center, "Presidential Speeches," "July 12, 1994: Remarks at the Brandenburg Gate," accessed December 22, 2018, https://millercenter.org/the-presidency/presidential-speeches/july-12-1994-remarks-brandenburg-gate.

2. Ibid.

3. Naomi Klein, *The Shock Doctrine: The Rise of Disaster Capitalism* (London: Picador, 2008).

4. Francis Fukuyama, *The End of History and the Last Man* (New York: Free Press, [1992] 2006).

5. T. H. Marshall, *Citizenship and Social Class: And Other Essays* (Cambridge: Cambridge University Press, 1950).

6. See Robert Reich, *Supercapitalism: The Transformation of Business, Democracy, and Everyday Life* (New York: Vintage, 2007).

7. For a broader theoretical conceptualization of these processes, see Cedric Robinson, *Black Marxism: The Making of the Black Radical Tradition* (Chapel Hill: University of North Carolina Press, 1983).

8. For an analysis of the U.S. case with a specific focus on social policy and gendered notions of fairness see Alice Kessler-Harris, *In Pursuit of Equity: Women, Men, and the Quest for Economic Citizenship in Twentieth-Century America* (Oxford: Oxford University Press, 2003)

9. We are building here on Karl Polanyi's idea of the double movement. The Hungarian economist and cultural anthropologist contended that there were some goods traded on markets that had not

been produced for that purpose ("fictitious commodities"). More specifically, he argued that treating money, land, and labor as commodities would ultimately backfire because using them up in the market would ultimately undermine the basic pillars of society. This is why at certain points in time, structural, spontaneous countermovements to processes of marketization were inevitable, leading to crises and political reactions so as to keep liberal market societies from unraveling. See Polanyi, *The Great Transformation: The Political and Economic Origins of Our Time* (Boston: Beacon, [1944] 2001).

10. Boris Vormann, *Global Port Cities in North America: Urbanization and Global Production Networks* (London: Routledge, 2015). See also Boris Vormann and Christian Lammert, eds., *Contours of the Illiberal State: Governing Circulation in the Smart Economy* (Frankfurt am Main: Campus, 2019).

11. Lisa Duggan, *The Twilight of Equality? Neoliberalism, Cultural Politics, and the Attack on Democracy* (New York: Beacon, 2003).

12. F. A. Hayek, *The Road to Serfdom: Text and Documents* (Chicago: University of Chicago Press, [1944] 2007).

13. Mark Levinson, *The Box: How the Shipping Container Made the World Smaller and the World Economy Bigger*, 2d ed. (Princeton, NJ: Princeton University Press, 2016).

14. Jamie Peck, *Constructions of Neoliberal Reason* (Oxford: Oxford University Press, 2010).

15. At the time, both sides of the political spectrum criticized bureaucracy. The Frankfurt School published vigorous diatribes against post–World War II state capitalism. While conservative narratives became dominant, left critiques lost a great deal of momentum after the 1970s. A recent book by David Graeber has been one of the rare attempts to formulate a progressive critique of bureaucracy. See Graeber, *The Utopia of Rules: On Technology, Stupidity, and the Secret Joys of Bureaucracy* (London: Melville House, 2015).

16. Milton Friedman, *Capitalism and Freedom* (Chicago: University of Chicago Press, [1962] 2002).

17. Ulrich Beck, *Risk Society: Towards a New Modernity* (Los Angeles: Sage, 1992); and Anthony Giddens, *Beyond Left and Right: The Future of Radical Politics* (Stanford, CA: Stanford University Press, 1994).

18. We tend to see external forces like this as inevitable, as being without any alternative. On one hand, this way of thinking about the economy and markets is quite naturally explained by political practice itself. Politicians who can claim that their hands are tied have an easier time defending their own positions against criticism (blame shifting). The notion of the market as an entity that is self-motivated, ties people's hands, and steers policy can already be found in the first liberal philosophers of the modern era, ever since John Locke, all of whom saw the market as a counterweight to absolutism. Later, Karl Marx also assumed that the economy could be described as obeying fixed laws. This understanding of the market reached its first peak in econometrics, which emerged in the early twentieth century and conceives the market as a phenomenon that can be mathematically modeled and follows laws not dissimilar to those of physics. This mathematization of social science research and way of thinking about the market has meanwhile spread to other disciplines and become part and parcel of common knowledge. For many people, it is not only this perception of markets, deeply anchored as it is in European political philosophy, that accounts for the tendency to view globalization as inevitable and hence without any alternative in the political realm. This sense is also supported by the fact that the driving force behind it appears to be technological innovation. From railroads to telegraph poles, from containers to computer technology, advances in communication and transportation technologies increase the mobility of people and goods and consequently appear to be the driving force behind globalization. And it all seems nonpolitical, since at first glance technological change appears to have little to do with politics.

19. Kenichi Ohmae, *The End of the Nation State: The Rise of Regional Economics* (New York: Free Press, 1996).

20. Fred Block and Margaret R. Somers, eds., *The Power of Market Fundamentalism: Karl Polanyi's Critique* (Cambridge, MA: Harvard University Press, 2014); and Fred Block, ed., *State of Innovation: The U.S. Government's Role in Technology Development* (London: Routledge, 2011).

21. See Mariana Mazzucato, *The Entrepreneurial State: Debunking Public vs. Private Sector Myths* (New York: Public Affairs, 2015).

22. Henrik Müller, "Auf dem Land regiert der Frust," *Der Spiegel*, July 31, 2016, accessed December 22, 2018, http://www.spiegel.de

/wirtschaft/soziales/stadt-und-land-wo-afd-donald-trump-le-pen-und
-co-stark-sind-a-1105526.html.

23. Gregor Aisch, Adam Pearce, and Karl Russell, "How Britain
Voted in the E.U. Referendum," updated June 24, 2016, accessed December
21, 2018, https://www.nytimes.com/interactive/2016/06/24/world
/europe/how-britain-voted-brexit-referendum.html.

24. Jesse A. Myerson, "Trumpism: It's Coming from the Suburbs,"
Nation, May 8, 2017, accessed December 21, 2018, https://www.thenation
.com/article/trumpism-its-coming-from-the-suburbs.

25. That the group of people who support Trump, Brexit, or the
Alternative for Germany does not consist solely of diehard right-wing,
xenophobic nationalists is also apparent from the fact that Syriza in
Greece, Occupy Wall Street in the United States, and Podemos in Spain
can also be conceived as progressive counterparts to global Trumpism.
These left-wing countermovements, amid social decline, also testify to
growing resistance to the crisis of liberalism.

26. University of Virginia, Miller Center, "Remarks at the Brandenburg Gate."

Chapter 3

1. *Economist*, Intelligence Unit Study, "Democracy Index 2016,"
accessed December 22, 2018,https://www.eiu.com/public/topical_report
.aspx?campaignid=DemocracyIndex2016.

2. Pew Research Center, U.S. Politics and Policy, "Beyond Distrust:
How Americans View Their Government," November 23, 2015, accessed
December 21, 2018, http://www.people-press.org/2015/11/23/beyond-dis
trust-how-americans-view-their-government.

3. Well-known expositions of the concept of American exceptionalism are offered by Louis Hartz, *The Liberal Tradition in America* (New
York: Harcourt, 1955); and Seymour Martin Lipset, *American Exceptionalism: A Double-Edged Sword* (New York: W. W. Norton, 1997). A
pertinent critique of the concept has been articulated by Donald Pease,
The New American Exceptionalism (Minneapolis: University of Minne-
sota Press, 2009).

4. Hans Morgenthau, *The Purpose of American Politics* (New York:
Alfred A. Knopf, 1960).

5. Roger Cohen, "America Unmasked," *New York Times*, April 24, 2009, accessed December 22, 2018, https://www.nytimes.com/2009/04/26/books/review/Cohen-t.html.

6. Robert N. Bellah, *The Broken Covenant: American Civil Religion in Time of Trial* (Chicago: University of Chicago Press, 1992).

7. Robert D. Putnam, *Making Democracy Work: Civic Traditions in Modern Italy* (Princeton, NJ: Princeton University Press, 1993).

8. Robert D. Putnam, *Bowling Alone: The Collapse and Revival of American Community* (New York: Simon & Schuster, 2000).

9. See Christian Lammert and Britta Grell, *Sozialpolitik in den USA: Eine Einführung* (Wiesbaden: Springer, 2012).

10. Michael B. Katz, *The Undeserving Poor: From the War on Poverty to the War on Welfare* (New York: Pantheon, 1989).

11. See Christopher Howard, *The Welfare State Nobody Knows: Debunking Myths About U.S. Social Policy* (Princeton, NJ: Princeton University Press, 2007); and Suzanne Mettler, *The Submerged State: How Invisible Government Politics Undermine American Democracy* (Chicago: University of Chicago Press, 2011). On the invisibility of contemporary statehood, also see Elizabeth Clemens, "Lineages of the Rube Goldberg State: Building and Blurring Public Programs, 1900–1940," in *Rethinking Political Institutions: The Art of the State*, ed. Ian Shapiro, Stephen Skowronek, and Daniel Galvin, 187–215 (New York: New York University Press, 2007). The implications of a visible welfare state, by contrast, are discussed in Andrea L. Campbell, *How Policies Make Citizens: Senior Citizen Activism and the American Welfare State* (Princeton, NJ: Princeton University Press, 2003).

12. Thomas Piketty, *Capital in the Twenty-First Century* (Cambridge, MA: Harvard University Press, 2014).

13. United States Census Bureau, Income and Poverty in the United States: 2014, U.S. Department of Commerce, 2015, accessed December 22, 2018, https://www.census.gov/content/dam/Census/library/publications/2015/demo/p60-252.pdf

14. Jacob Hacker and Paul Pierson, *American Amnesia: How the War on Government Led Us to Forget What Made America Prosper* (New York: Simon & Schuster, 2016).

15. Elise Gould, "The State of American Wages 2017," Economic Policy Institute, March 1, 2018, accessed December 22, 2018, https://

www.epi.org/publication/the-state-of-american-wages-2017-wages
-have-finally-recovered-from-the-blow-of-the-great-recession-but-are
-still-growing-too-slowly-and-unequally/#epi-toc-8.

16. Martin Gilens and Benjamin Page, "Testing Theories of American Politics: Elites, Interest Groups, and Average Citizens," *Perspectives in Politics* 12, no. 3 (2014), 564–81; Martin Gilens, *Affluence and Influence: Economic Inequality and Political Power in America* (Princeton, NJ: Princeton University Press, 2012).

17. On polarization see Alan S. Gerber and Eric Schickler, eds., *Governing in a Polarized Age: Elections, Parties, and Political Representation in America* (Cambridge: Cambridge University Press, 2017); Sean M. Theriault, *Party Polarization in Congress* (Cambridge: Cambridge University Press, 2008); and Barbara Sinclair, *Party Wars: Polarization and the Politics of National Policy-Making* (Norman: University of Oklahoma Press, 2006).

18. W. Lance Bennett, Alexandra Segerberg, and Curd Knüpfer, "The Democratic Interface: Technology, Political Organization, and Diverging Patterns of Electoral Representation," *Information, Communication and Society* 1 (2018), 1–26.

Chapter 4

1. T. R. Reid, *The United States of Europe: The New Superpower and the End of American Supremacy* (New York: Penguin, 2004).

2. From $9.8 trillion in 2002 to $19.1 trillion in 2008 (both in current U.S. dollars). See World Bank Data, "European Union," accessed December 21, 2018, http://data.worldbank.org/region/european-union.

3. Timothy Garton Ash, *Facts Are Subversive: Political Writing from a Decade Without a Name* (New Haven, CT: Yale University Press, 2010), 141.

4. Infratest-dimap (website), "ARD Deutschlandtrend," accessed December 21, 2018, http://www.infratest-dimap.de/umfragen-analysen/bundesweit/ard-deutschlandtrend/2016/september.

5. Boris Vormann, *Zwischen alter und neuer Welt: Nationenbildung im transatlantischen Raum* (Heidelberg: Synchron, 2012).

6. Hans-Jürgen Puhle, "Das atlantische Syndrom: Europa, Amerika und der 'Westen,'" *Geschichte und Gesellschaft* 22 (2006), 179–99.

7. Hans Braun, "Helmut Schelskys Konzept der ‚nivellierten Mittelstandsgesellschaft' und die Bundesrepublik der 50er Jahre," *Archiv für Sozialgeschichte* 29 (1989), 199–223; Ulrich Beck, *Risk Society: Towards a New Modernity* (Los Angeles: Sage, 1992).

8. The European Commission's so-called Eurobarometer surveys public opinion over the past decades and is available at http://ec.europa .eu/commfrontoffice/publicopinion/index.cfm, accessed December 21, 2018.

9. "An Overview of Growing Income Inequalities in OECD Countries: Main Findings," in OECD, *Divided We Stand: Why Inequality Keeps Rising* (2011) 32, accessed December 22, 2018, https://www.oecd .org/els/soc/49499779.pdf.

10. Translated from the German original. For details see the afterword in Mark Blyth, *Wie Europa sich kaputtspart: Die gescheiterte Idee der Austeritätspolitik* (Bonn: Dietz, 2014), S. 341ff.

11. OECD, *In It Together: Why Less Inequality Benefits All* (Paris: OECD, 2015).

12. Eurofound, "Income Inequalities and Employment Patterns in Europe Before and After the Great Recession" (Luxembourg: Publications Office of the European Union, 2017), 30, Fig. 11, accessed December 22, 2018, https://www.eurofound.europa.eu/sites/default/files/ef _publication/field_ef_document/ef1663en.pdf.

13. Excellent analyses of the financial crisis by leading social scientists are collected in a trilogy by Craig Calhoun and Georgi Derluguian, eds., *Business as Usual: The Roots of the Global Financial Meltdown*; *The Deepening Crisis: Governance Challenges After Neoliberalism*; and *Aftermath: A New Global Economic Order?* (New York: New York University Press, 2011).

14. Citation translated from Tagesschau.de (website), "Die Konjunktur kippt," November 2008, accessed December 22, 2018, https://www.tagesschau.de/wirtschaft/chronologiefinanzmarktkrise 108.html.

15. "Commerzbank muss 17 Millionen Euro Bußgeld bezahlen," in *Handelsblatt*, January 16, 2016, accessed December 22, 2018, http:// www.handelsblatt.com/finanzen/banken-versicherungen/beihilfe-zur -steuerhinterziehung-commerzbank-muss-17-millionen-euro-bussgeld -zahlen/12839844.html.

16. Richard H. Thaler and Cass R. Sunstein, *Nudge: Improving Decisions About Health, Wealth and Happiness* (London: Penguin, 2009); and Daniel Kahneman, *Thinking, Fast and Slow* (London: Penguin, 2012).

17. Edmund L. Andrews, "Greenspan Concedes Error on Regulation," *New York Times*, October 23, 2008, accessed December 22, 2018, available at https://www.nytimes.com/2008/10/24/business/economy /24panel.html.

18. OECD, Growing Unequal? Income Distribution and Poverty in OECD Countries, Paris 2008, accessed December 22, 2018, https:// www.oecd.org/els/soc/41527936.pdf; OECD, Divided We Stand: Why Inequality Keeps Rising, Paris 2011, accessed December 22, 2018, https:// www.oecd.org/els/soc/49170768.pdf; OECD, In It Together: Why Less Inequality Benefits All, Paris 2013, accessed, December 22, 2018, https:// www.oecd.org/els/soc/OECD2015-In-It-Together-Chapter1-Overview -Inequality.pdf.

19. Mark Blyth, *Austerity: The History of a Dangerous Idea* (Oxford: Oxford University Press, 2013). For an analysis that explores the role of austerity policies in the case of Brexit see Jonathan Hopkin, "When Polanyi Met Farage: Market Fundamentalism, Economic Nationalism, and Britain's Exit from the European Union," *British Journal of Politics and International Relations* 19 (2017), 465–78. For the broader European context see Jonathan Hopkin and Mark Blyth, "The Global Economics of European Populism: Growth Regimes and Party System Change in Europe," *Government and Opposition* (2018), 1–33.

20. Paul Krugman, "That '30s Feeling," *New York Times*, June 17, 2010, accessed December 22, 2018, http://www.nytimes.com/2010/06/18 /opinion/18krugman.html?hp&_r=0.

21. Frank Vandebroucke and David Rinaldi, "Soziale Ungleichheit in Europa: Die Herausforderungen Konvergenz und Kohäsion," Bertelsmann Stiftung Graue Publikationen, 2016, accessed December 22, 2018, https://www.bertelsmann-stiftung.de/fileadmin/files/BSt /Publikationen/GrauePublikationen/Studie_IFT_Soziale_Ungleichheit _in_Europa_2016.pdf.

22. Cited passages are translated from the German original. Oxfam Germany (website), "Ungleichheit und Armut in Europa," September 8, 2015, accessed December 22, 2018, https://www.oxfam.de

/presse/pressemitteilungen/2015-09-08-oxfam-bericht-ungleichheit
-armut-europa-bedrohen-sozialen.

23. Ibid.

24. For 2012, see Oliver Das Gupta, "Geschönter Armutsbericht," *Süddeutsche Zeitung*, November 28, 2012, http://www.sueddeutsche .de/politik/geschoenter-armutsbericht-opposition-wirft-merkels -koalition-vertuschung-vor-1.1535451; for 2013, see "Opposition wirft Schwarz-Gelb Zensur vor," *Zeit Online*, February 21, 2013, http://www .zeit.de/politik/deutschland/2013-02/bundestagsdebatte-armuts-und -reichtumsbericht; for 2016, see "Bundesregierung strich offenbar heikle Passagen," *Handelsblatt*, December 15, 2016, http://www.handelsblatt.com /politik/deutschland/armutsbericht-bundesregierung-strich-offenbar -heikle-passagen/14987286.html; for 2017, see Christoph Butterwegge, "Wer arm ist, zählt wenig," *Deutschlandfunk Kultur*, April 12, 2017, http:// www.deutschlandfunkkultur.de/der-geschoente-armutsbericht-der -bundesregierung-wer-arm.1005.de.html?dram:article_id=383639, all accessed December 21, 2018.

25. Daniel Schraad-Tischler and Christof Schiller, *Social Justice in the EU: Index Report 2016—Social Inclusion Monitor Europe* (Gütersloh, Germany: Bertelsmann Stiftung, 2016).

26. See Eurofound, "Income Inequalities."

27. "The Gap Between Poor and Rich Regions in Europe Is Widening," *Economist*, October 27, 2016, accessed December 22, 2018, http:// www.economist.com/news/europe/21709336-austerity-partly-blame -gap-between-poor-and-rich-regions-europe-widening.

28. European Commission, "Eurobarometer 85," 125, 129.

29. European Commission, "Eurobarometer 2013."

30. Hans-Jürgen Schlamp, "Fatales Studienergebnis: Europa glaubt nicht mehr an Europa," *Der Spiegel*, February 25, 2015, accessed December 22, 2018, http://www.spiegel.de/politik/ausland/eu-studie-buerger -haben-kein-vertrauen-in-europa-a-1017155.html.

31. "Europe's Deadly Paralysis on Migration," *New York Times*, July 3, 2017, accessed December 21, 2018, https://www.nytimes.com/2017/07 /03/opinion/europes-deadly-paralysis-on-migration.html?smprod= nytcore-ipad&smid=nytcore-ipad-share&_r=0.

32. European Commission, "Eurobarometer 85," S. 124f.

Chapter 5

1. Ralf Fücks, *Freiheit verteidigen: Wie wir den Kampf um die offene Gesellschaft gewinnen* (Munich: Carl Hanser, 2017).

2. Benjamin E. Page and Lawrence R. Jacobs, *Class War? What Americans Really Think About Economic Inequality* (Chicago: University of Chicago Press, 2009).

3. Karl Polanyi, *The Great Transformation: The Political and Economic Origins of Our Time* (Boston: Beacon, [1944] 2001).

4. Ernest Renan, "What Is a Nation?" in *Becoming National: A Reader*, ed. Geoff Eley and Ronald Grigor Suny, 42–55 (Oxford: Oxford University Press, [1882] 1996).

5. Craig Calhoun, *Nations Matter. Culture, History, and the Cosmopolitan Dream* (New York: Routledge, 2007), 1.

6. Germany's defense minister Ursula von der Leyen is a prominent supporter of this idea, but she is part of a longer-standing discourse on the role of security policy in identity formation. See, for instance, Karl-Heinz Kamp, "Europäische Sicherheitspolitik in der Krise," in *Beiträge zur internationalen Politik und Sicherheit* 1 (2005), accessed December 22, 2018, http://www.kas.de/upload/dokumente/trans_portal/bips_kamp.pdf.

7. Frank Vandebroucke and David Rinaldi, "Soziale Ungleichheit in Europa: Die Herausforderungen Konvergenz und Kohäsion," Bertelsmann Stiftung Graue Publikationen, accessed December 22, 2018, https://www.bertelsmann-stiftung.de/fileadmin/files/BSt/Publikationen/GrauePublikationen/Studie_IFT_Soziale_Ungleichheit_in_Europa_2016.pdf.

8. For inspiration in this regard, read Craig Calhoun, *Nations Matter: Culture, History, and the Cosmopolitan Dream* (London: Routledge, 2007).

9. See Mariana Mazzucato, *The Entrepreneurial State: Debunking Public vs. Private Sector Myths* (New York: Public Affairs, 2015) for a groundbreaking study on active statehood with a focus on public investments in Research and Development (R&D). For a typology and comparative historical analyses of state interventions in globalization processes see Boris Vormann and Christian Lammert, *Contours of the*

Illiberal State: Governing Circulation in the Smart Economy (Frankfurt am Main: Campus, 2019).

10. Even if, of course, "world systems" existed before the twentieth century, the transatlantic slave trade being perhaps the most prominent example.

11. Robert Heilbroner, *The Nature and Logic of Capitalism* (New York: Norton, 1986).

12. Colin Crouch engages this question in detail in *Post-Democracy* (Cambridge: Polity, 2004).

13. Saskia Sassen, *The Global City: New York, London, Tokyo* (Princeton, NJ: Princeton University Press, 1991). See also Peter J. Taylor, *World City Network: A Global Urban Analysis* (London: Routledge, 2004); and Roger Keil and Rianne Mahon, *Leviathan Undone? Towards a Political Economy of Scale* (Vancouver: UBC, 2009).

14. Naomi Klein, *No Is Not Enough: Defeating the New Shock Politics* (London: Allen Lane, 2017).

15. Cornelia Daheim and Ole Winkelmann, "2050: Die Zukunft der Arbeit," Bertelsmann Stiftung, accessed December 21, 2018, https://www.bertelsmann-stiftung.de/fileadmin/files/BSt/Publikationen/GrauePublikationen/BST_Delphi_Studie_2016.pdf.

16. Carl Frey and Michael Osborne, "The Future of Employment: How Susceptible Are Jobs to Computerisation?" in *Oxford Martine Programme Working Paper*, September 17, 2013, accessed December 21, 2018, http://www.oxfordmartin.ox.ac.uk/downloads/academic/The_Future_of_Employment.pdf.

17. John Maynard Keynes published his piece "Economic Possibilities for our Grandchildren" in 1930. It can be found in the following volume: John Maynard Keynes, *Essays in Persuasion* (New York: W. W. Norton, 1963), 358–73. David Graeber's argument was first published as a short article, which the author then turned into a full-fledged monograph with the title *Bullshit Jobs: A Theory* (London: Allen Lane, 2018).

18. For instance, Wolfgang Merkel makes such a fatalist argument in a newspaper article on the future of democracy with the title "Krise? Krise!" (*Frankfurter Allgemeine Zeitung*, May 5, 2013, accessed December 22, 2018, http://www.faz.net/aktuell/politik/die-gegenwart/zukunft

-der-demokratie-krise-krise-12173238.html?printPagedArticle=true #pageIndex_2).

19. This debate was initiated in part by James N. Rosenau and Ernst-Otto Czempiel, eds., *Governance Without Government: Order and Change in World Politics* (Cambridge: Cambridge University Press, 1992).

20. Jürgen Habermas, "Hat die Konstitutionalisierung des Völkerrechts noch eine Chance?" in *Der gespaltene Westen: Kleine politische Schriften X*, ed. Jürgen Habermas, 113–93 (Frankfurt am Main: Suhrkamp, 2004).

21. Ingeborg Gabriel, "Zur Zukunft der Demokratie unter Globalisierungsbedingungen: Eine sozialethische Problemanzeige, " *Jahrbuch für Christliche Sozialwissenschaften* 54 (2013), 83–104, 92.

22. The problem of technological rationality is not new. Herbert Marcuse articulated a decisive contribution in *One-Dimensional Man: Studies in the Ideology of Advanced Industrial Society* (Boston: Beacon, 1964).

23. See Evgeny Mozorov, *To Save Everything, Click Here: The Folly of Technological Solutionism* (New York: Public Affairs, 2013).

24. Stephen Graham and Simon Marvin, *Splintering Urbanism* (London: Routledge, 2001).

25. Neil Brenner and Christian Schmid, "Towards a New Epistemology of the Urban?" *CITY* 19 (2015), 151–82. See also Hillary Angelo and David Wachsmuth, "Urbanizing Political Ecology: A Critique of Methodological Cityism," *International Journal of Urban and Regional Research* 39 (2015), 16–27.

26. Curd Knüpfer, Lance Bennett, and Alexandra Segerberg, "The Democratic Interface: Technology, Political Organization, and Diverging Patterns of Electoral Representation," *Information, Communication and Sociology* 21 (2017), 1–26.

27. On the public role of universities, see Craig Calhoun, "The University and the Public Good," *Thesis Eleven* 84 (2006), 7–43.

Acknowledgments

The authors would like to thank Susan H. Gillespie for her outstanding translation and her extremely generous support in this project. It would not have taken off without her. We are also indebted to Damon Linker for his help throughout the publication process. We thank him and Patricia Wieland for the excellent editing of the final text. Franziska Riel has been very helpful in crafting the manuscript; Inka Ihmels and Franziska Günther at Aufbau Verlag have facilitated this English-language version of our book. Our thanks also go to Sandy Zipp for establishing the contact to the University of Pennsylvania Press and making this publication possible in the first place. Moreover, we are grateful to the institutions that allowed us to conduct our research and writing: Bard College Berlin, the John-F.-Kennedy Institute for North American Studies at Freie Universität Berlin, and Deutsches Haus at New York University. Finally, we would like to thank our colleagues and friends Hillary Angelo, Helmut Aust, Jonathan Becker, Roger Berkowitz, Mark Blyth, Craig Calhoun, Gabriella Etmeksoglou, Ruth Wilson Gilmore, Stefan Höhne,

Acknowledgments

Jonathan Hopkin, Alice Kessler Harris, Curd Knüpfer, Ingo Kolboom, Margit Mayer, Christoph Raetzsch, Markus B. Siewert, Tomasz Stompor, David Wachsmuth, Rosemary Wakeman, and Michael Weinman for the inspiring encounters and exchanges over the years. Their support and friendship have been an extraordinary gift.